WITHDRAWN

ACROSS THE PLAINS

ACROSS THE PLAINS

WITH OTHER

MEMORIES AND ESSAYS

BY

ROBERT LOUIS STEVENSON

NEW YORK
CHARLES SCRIBNER'S SONS
1901

TO PAUL BOURGET.

TRAVELLER and student and curious as you are, you will never have heard the name of Vailima, most likely not even that of Upolu, and Samoa itself may be strange to your ears. To these barbaric seats there came the other day a yellow book with your name on the title, and filled in every page with the exquisite gifts of your art. Let me take and change your own words: *J'ai beau admirer les autres de toutes mes forces, c'est avec vous que je me complais à vivre.*

R. L. S.

VAILIMA,
   UPOLU,
      SAMOA.

LETTER TO THE AUTHOR

My Dear Stevenson,

You have trusted me with the choice and arrangement of these papers, written before you departed to the South Seas, and have asked me to add a preface to the volume. But it is your prose the public wish to read, not mine; and I am sure they will willingly be spared the preface. Acknowledgments are due in your name to the publishers of the several magazines from which the papers are collected, viz. *Fraser's*, *Longman's*, the *Magazine of Art*, and *Scribner's*. I will only add, lest any reader should find the tone of the concluding pieces less inspiriting than your wont, that they were written under circumstances of especial gloom

Preface

and sickness. 'I agree with you the lights seem a little turned down,' so you write to me now; 'the truth is I was far through, and came none too soon to the South Seas, where I was to recover peace of body and mind. And however low the lights, the stuff is true. . . .' Well, inasmuch as the South Sea sirens have breathed new life into you, we are bound to be heartily grateful to them, though as they keep you so far removed from us, it is difficult not to bear them a grudge; and if they would reconcile us quite, they have but to do two things more — to teach you new tales that shall charm us like your old, and to spare you, at least once in a while in summer, to climates within reach of us who are task-bound for ten months in the year beside the Thames.

Yours ever,

SIDNEY COLVIN.

February, 1892

CONTENTS

I

ACROSS THE PLAINS:

LEAVES FROM THE NOTEBOOK OF AN EMI-GRANT BETWEEN NEW YORK AND SAN FRANCISCO

MONDAY.—It was, if I remember rightly, five o'clock when we were all signalled to be present at the Ferry Depôt of the railroad. An emigrant ship had arrived at New York on the Saturday night, another on the Sunday morning, our own on Sunday afternoon, a fourth early on Monday; and as there is no emigrant train on Sunday, a great part of the passengers from these four ships was concentrated on the train by which I was to travel. There was a babel of bewildered men, women, and children. The wretched little booking office, and the baggage-room, which was not much larger, were crowded thick with emigrants, and were heavy and rank with the atmosphere of dripping clothes. Open carts full of bedding stood by the half-hour in the rain. The officials loaded each other with recriminations. A bearded, mildewed little man, whom I take to have been an emigrant agent, was all over the place, his mouth full of brimstone, blustering and interfering. It was plain that the whole system, if system there was, had utterly broken down under the strain of so many passengers.

My own ticket was given me at once, and an oldish man, who preserved his head in the midst of this turmoil, got my baggage registered, and counselled me to stay quietly where I was till he should give me the word to move. I had taken along with me a small valise, a knapsack, which I carried on my shoulders, and in the bag of my railway rug the whole of *Bancroft's History of the United States*, in six fat volumes. It was as much as I could carry with convenience even for short distances, but it insured me plenty of clothing, and the valise was at that moment, and often after, useful for a stool. I am sure I sat for an hour in the baggage-room, and wretched enough it was; yet, when at last the word was passed to me and I picked up my bundles and got under way, it was only to exchange discomfort for downright misery and danger.

I followed the porters into a long shed reaching downhill from West Street to the river. It was dark, the wind blew clean through it from end to end; and here I found a great block of passengers and baggage, hundreds of one and tons of the other. I feel I shall have a difficulty to make myself believed; and certainly the scene must have been exceptional, for it was too dangerous for daily repetition. It was a tight jam; there was no fair way through the mingled mass of brute and living obstruction. Into the upper skirts of the crowd porters, infuriated by hurry and overwork, clove their way with shouts. I may say that we stood like sheep, and that the porters charged among us like so many maddened sheep-dogs; and I believe these men were no longer answerable for their acts. It

mattered not what they were carrying, they
drove straight into the press, and when they
could get no farther, blindly discharged their
barrowful. With my own hand, for instance,
I saved the life of a child as it sat upon its
mother's knee, she sitting on a box; and since I
heard of no accident, I must suppose that there
were many similar interpositions in the course
of the evening. It will give some idea of the
state of mind to which we were reduced if I
tell you that neither the porter nor the mother
of the child paid the least attention to my act.
It was not till some time after that I understood what I had done myself, for to ward off
heavy boxes seemed at the moment a natural
incident of human life. Cold, wet, clamour,
dead opposition to progress, such as one en-
counters in an evil dream, had utterly daunted
the spirits. We had accepted this purgatory
as a child accepts the conditions of the world.
For my part, I shivered a little, and my back
ached wearily; but I believe I had neither a
hope nor a fear, and all the activities of my
nature had become tributary to one massive
sensation of discomfort.

At length, and after how long an interval
I hesitate to guess, the crowd began to move,
heavily straining through itself. About the
same time some lamps were lighted, and threw
a sudden flare over the shed. We were being
filtered out into the river boat for Jersey City.
You may imagine how slowly this filtering
proceeded, through the dense, choking crush,
every one overladen with packages or children,
and yet under the necessity of fishing out his
ticket by the way; but it ended at length for
me, and I found myself on deck under a flimsy
awning and with a trifle of elbow-room to
stretch and breathe in. This was on the star-
board; for the bulk of the emigrants stuck
hopelessly on the port side, by which we had
entered. In vain the seamen shouted to them
to move on, and threatened them with ship-
wreck. These poor people were under a spell
of stupor, and did not stir a foot. It rained as
heavily as ever, but the wind now came in
sudden claps and capfuls, not without danger
to a boat so badly ballasted as ours; and we
crept over the river in the darkness, trailing
one paddle in the water like a wounded duck,

and passed ever and again by huge, illuminated steamers running many knots, and heralding their approach by strains of music. The contrast between these pleasure embarkations and our own grim vessel, with her list to port and her freight of wet and silent emigrants, was of that glaring description which we count too obvious for the purposes of art.

The landing at Jersey City was done in a stampede. I had a fixed sense of calamity, and to judge by conduct, the same persuasion was common to us all. A panic selfishness, like that produced by fear, presided over the disorder of our landing. People pushed, and elbowed, and ran, the families following how they could. Children fell, and were picked up to be rewarded by a blow. One child, who had lost her parents, screamed steadily and with increasing shrillness, as though verging towards a fit; an official kept her by him, but no one else seemed so much as to remark her distress; and I am ashamed to say that I ran among the rest. I was so weary that I had twice to make a halt and set down my bundles in the hundred yards or so between the pier and the railway station, so that I was quite wet by the time that I got under cover. There was no waiting-room, no refreshment room; the cars were locked; and for at least another hour, or so it seemed, we had to camp upon the draughty, gaslit platform. I sat on my valise, too crushed to observe my neighbours; but as they were all cold, and wet, and weary, and driven stupidly crazy by the mismanagement to which we had been subjected, I believe they can have been no happier than myself. I bought half a dozen oranges from a boy, for oranges and nuts were the only refection to be had. As only two of them had even a pretence of juice, I threw the other four under the cars, and beheld, as in a dream, grown people and children groping on the track after my leavings.

At last we were admitted into the cars, utterly dejected, and far from dry. For my own part, I got out a clothes-brush, and brushed my trousers as hard as I could till I had dried them and warmed my blood into the bargain; but no one else, except my next neighbour to whom I lent the brush, appeared to take the least precaution. As they were, they composed themselves to sleep. I had seen the lights of Philadelphia, and been twice ordered to change carriages and twice counter-manded, before I allowed myself to follow their example.

Tuesday.—When I awoke, it was already day; the train was standing idle; I was in the last carriage, and, seeing some others strolling to and fro about the lines, I opened the door and stepped forth, as from a caravan by the wayside. We were near no station, nor even, as far as I could see, within reach of any signal. A green, open, undulating country stretched away upon all sides. Locust trees and a single field of Indian corn gave it a foreign grace and interest; but the contours of the land were soft and English. It was not quite England, neither was it quite France; yet like enough either to seem natural in my eyes. And it was in the sky, and not upon the earth, that I was surprised to find a change. Explain it how you may, and for my part I cannot explain it at all, the sun rises with a different splendour in America and Europe. There is more clear gold and scarlet in our old country mornings; more purple, brown, and smoky orange in those of the new. It may be from habit, but to me the coming of day is less fresh and inspiriting in the latter; it has a duskier glory, and more nearly resembles sunset; it seems to fit some subsequential, evening epoch of the world, as though America were in fact, and not merely in fancy, farther from the orient of Aurora and the springs of day. I thought so then, by the railroad side in Pennsylvania, and I have thought so a dozen times since in far distant parts of the continent. If it be an illusion it is one very deeply rooted, and in which my eyesight is accomplice.

Soon after a train whisked by, announcing and accompanying its passage by the swift beating of a sort of chapel bell upon the engine; and as it was for this we had been waiting, we were summoned by the cry of 'All aboard!' and went on again upon our way. The whole line, it appeared, was topsy-turvy; an accident at midnight having thrown all the traffic hours into arrear. We paid for this in the flesh, for we had no meals all that day. Fruit we could buy upon the cars; and now and then we had a few minutes at some station with a meagre show of rolls and sandwiches for sale; but we were so many and so ravenous that, though I tried at every opportunity, the coffee was always exhausted before I could elbow my way to the counter.

Our American sunrise had ushered in a noble summer's day. There was not a cloud; the sunshine was baking; yet in the woody river valleys among which we wound our way, the atmosphere preserved a sparkling freshness till late in the afternoon. It had an inland sweetness and variety to one newly from the sea; it smelt of woods, rivers, and the delved earth. These, though in so far a country, were airs from home. I stood on the platform by the hour; and as I saw, one after another, pleasant villages, carts upon the highway and fishers by the stream, and heard cockcrows and cheery voices in the distance, and beheld the sun, no longer shining blankly on the plains of ocean, but striking among shapely hills and his light dispersed and coloured by a thousand accidents of form and surface, I began to exult with myself upon this rise in life like a man who had come into a rich estate. And when I had asked the name of a river from the brakesman, and heard that it was called the Susquehanna, the beauty of the name seemed to be part and parcel of the beauty of the land. As when Adam with divine fitness named the creatures, so this word Susquehanna was at once accepted by the fancy. That was the name, as no other could be, for that shining river and desirable valley.

None can care for literature in itself who do not take a special pleasure in the sound of names; and there is no part of the world where nomenclature is so rich, poetical, humorous, and picturesque as the United States of America. All times, races, and languages have brought their contribution. Pekin is in the same State with Euclid, with Bellefontaine, and with Sandusky. Chelsea, with its London associations of red brick, Sloane Square, and the King's Road, is own suburb to stately and primeval Memphis; there they have their seat, translated names of cities, where the Mississippi runs by

Tennessee and Arkansas;[1] and both, while I was crossing the continent, lay, watched by armed men, in the horror and isolation of a plague. Old, red Manhattan lies, like an Indian arrowhead under a steam factory, below anglified New York. The names of the States and Territories themselves form a chorus of sweet and most romantic vocables: Delaware, Ohio, Indiana, Florida, Dakota, Iowa, Wyoming, Minnesota, and the Carolinas; there are few poems with a nobler music for the ear: a songful, tuneful land; and if the new Homer shall arise from the Western continent, his verse will be enriched, his pages sing spontaneously, with the names of states and cities that would strike the fancy in a business circular.

Late in the evening we were landed in a waiting-room at Pittsburg. I had now under my charge a young and sprightly Dutch widow with her children; these I was to watch over providentially for a certain distance farther on the way; but as I found she was furnished with a basket of eatables, I left her in the waiting-room to seek a dinner for myself.

[1] Please pronounce Arkansaw, with the accent on the first.

I mention this meal, not only because it was the first of which I had partaken for about thirty hours, but because it was the means of my first introduction to a coloured gentleman. He did me the honour to wait upon me after a fashion, while I was eating; and with every word, look, and gesture marched me farther into the country of surprise. He was indeed strikingly unlike the negroes of Mrs. Beecher Stowe, or the Christy Minstrels of my youth. Imagine a gentleman, certainly somewhat dark, but of a pleasant warm hue, speaking English with a slight and rather odd foreign accent, every inch a man of the world, and armed with manners so patronisingly superior that I am at a loss to name their parallel in England. A butler perhaps rides as high over the unbutlered, but then he sets you right with a reserve and a sort of sighing patience which one is often moved to admire. And again, the abstract butler never stoops to familiarity. But the coloured gentleman will pass you a wink at a time; he is familiar like an upper form boy to a fag; he unbends to you like Prince Hal with Poins and Falstaff. He makes himself at home

and welcome. Indeed, I may say, this waiter
behaved himself to me throughout that supper
much as, with us, a young, free, and not very
self-respecting master might behave to a good-
looking chambermaid. I had come prepared to
pity the poor negro, to put him at his ease, to
prove in a thousand condescensions that I was
no sharer in the prejudice of race; but I assure
you I put my patronage away for another
occasion, and had the grace to be pleased with
that result.

Seeing he was a very honest fellow, I con-
sulted him upon a point of etiquette: if one
should offer to tip the American waiter?
Certainly not, he told me. Never. It would
not do. They considered themselves too highly
to accept. They would even resent the offer.
As for him and me, we had enjoyed a very
pleasant conversation; he, in particular, had
found much pleasure in my society; I was a
stranger; this was exactly one of those rare
conjunctures. . . . Without being very clear
seeing, I can still perceive the sun at noonday;
and the coloured gentleman deftly pocketed a
quarter.

Wednesday.—A little after midnight I con-
voyed my widow and orphans on board the
train; and morning found us far into Ohio.
This had early been a favourite home of my
imagination; I have played at being in Ohio
by the week, and enjoyed some capital sport
there with a dummy gun, my person being still
unbreeched. My preference was founded on a
work which appeared in *Cassell's Family Paper*,
and was read aloud to me by my nurse. It
narrated the doings of one Custaloga, an Indian
brave, who, in the last chapter, very obligingly
washed the paint off his face and became Sir
Reginald Somebody-or-other; a trick I never
forgave him. The idea of a man being an
Indian brave, and then giving that up to be a
baronet, was one which my mind rejected. It
offended verisimilitude, like the pretended anxiety of Robinson Crusoe and others to escape
from uninhabited islands.

But Ohio was not at all as I had pictured
it. We were now on those great plains which
stretch unbroken to the Rocky Mountains.
The country was flat like Holland, but far from
being dull. All through Ohio, Indiana, Illinois,

and Iowa, or for as much as I saw of them from
the train and in my waking moments, it was
rich and various, and breathed an elegance
peculiar to itself. The tall corn pleased the
eye; the trees were graceful in themselves, and
framed the plain into long, aërial vistas; and
the clean, bright, gardened townships spoke of
country fare and pleasant summer evenings on
the stoop. It was a sort of flat paradise; but,
I am afraid, not unfrequented by the devil.
That morning dawned with such a freezing
chill as I have rarely felt; a chill that was not
perhaps so measurable by instrument, as it
struck home upon the heart and seemed to
travel with the blood. Day came in with a
shudder. White mists lay thinly over the surface of the plain, as we see them more often on
a lake; and though the sun had soon dispersed
and drunk them up, leaving an atmosphere of
fever heat and crystal pureness from horizon to
horizon, the mists had still been there, and we
knew that this paradise was haunted by killing
damps and foul malaria. The fences along the
line bore but two descriptions of advertisement;
one to recommend tobaccos, and the other to

vaunt remedies against the ague. At the point of day, and while we were all in the grasp of that first chill, a native of the state, who had got in at some way station, pronounced it, with a doctoral air, 'a fever and ague morning.'

The Dutch widow was a person of some character. She had conceived at first sight a great aversion for the present writer, which she was at no pains to conceal. But being a woman of a practical spirit, she made no difficulty about accepting my attentions, and encouraged me to buy her children fruits and candies, to carry all her parcels, and even to sleep upon the floor that she might profit by my empty seat. Nay, she was such a rattle by nature, and so powerfully moved to autobiographical talk, that she was forced, for want of a better, to take me into confidence and tell me the story of her life. I heard about her late husband, who seemed to have made his chief impression by taking her out pleasuring on Sundays. I could tell you her prospects, her hopes, the amount of her fortune, the cost of her housekeeping by the week, and a variety of particular matters that are not usually disclosed

except to friends. At one station, she shook
up her children to look at a man on the platform and say if he were not like Mr. Z.;
while to me she explained how she had been
keeping company with this Mr. Z., how far
matters had proceeded, and how it was because
of his desistance that she was now travelling to
the west. Then, when I was thus put in
possession of the facts, she asked my judgment
on that type of manly beauty. I admired it
to her heart's content. She was not, I think,
remarkably veracious in talk, but broidered as
fancy prompted, and built castles in the air out
of her past; yet she had that sort of candour,
to keep me, in spite of all these confidences,
steadily aware of her aversion. Her parting
words were ingeniously honest. 'I am sure,'
said she, 'we all *ought* to be very much obliged
to you.' I cannot pretend that she put me at
my ease; but I had a certain respect for such a
genuine dislike. A poor nature would have
slipped, in the course of these familiarities, into
a sort of worthless toleration for me.

We reached Chicago in the evening. I was
turned out of the cars, bundled into an omnibus,

and driven off through the streets to the station of a different railroad. Chicago seemed a great and gloomy city. I remember having subscribed, let us say sixpence, towards its restoration at the period of the fire; and now when I beheld street after street of ponderous houses and crowds of comfortable burghers, I thought it would be a graceful act for the corporation to refund that sixpence, or, at the least, to entertain me to a cheerful dinner. But there was no word of restitution. I was that city's benefactor, yet I was received in a third-class waiting-room, and the best dinner I could get was a dish of ham and eggs at my own expense.

I can safely say, I have never been so dog-tired as that night in Chicago. When it was time to start, I descended the platform like a man in a dream. It was a long train, lighted from end to end; and car after car, as I came up with it, was not only filled but overflowing. My valise, my knapsack, my rug, with those six ponderous tomes of Bancroft, weighed me double; I was hot, feverish, painfully athirst; and there was a great darkness over me, an internal darkness, not to be dispelled by gas. When at last I found an empty bench, I sank into it like a bundle of rags, the world seemed to swim away into the distance, and my consciousness dwindled within me to a mere pin's head, like a taper on a foggy night.

When I came a little more to myself, I found that there had sat down beside me a very cheerful, rosy little German gentleman, somewhat gone in drink, who was talking away to me, nineteen to the dozen, as they say. I did my best to keep up the conversation; for it seemed to me dimly as if something depended upon that. I heard him relate, among many other things, that there were pickpockets on the train, who had already robbed a man of forty dollars and a return ticket; but though I caught the words, I do not think I properly understood the sense until next morning; and I believe I replied at the time that I was very glad to hear it. What else he talked about I have no guess; I remember a gabbling sound of words, his profuse gesticulation, and his smile, which was highly explanatory; but no more. And I suppose I must have shown my confusion very plainly; for, first, I saw him knit his brows at me like one who has conceived a doubt; next, he tried me in German, supposing perhaps that I was unfamiliar with the English tongue; and finally, in despair, he rose and left me. I felt chagrined; but my fatigue was too crushing for delay, and, stretching myself as far as that was possible upon the bench, I was received at once into a dreamless stupor.

The little German gentleman was only going a little way into the suburbs after a *diner fin*, and was bent on entertainment while the journey lasted. Having failed with me, he pitched next upon another emigrant, who had come through from Canada, and was not one jot less weary than myself. Nay, even in a natural state, as I found next morning when we scraped acquaintance, he was a heavy, uncommunicative man. After trying him on different topics, it appears that the little German gentleman flounced into a temper, swore an oath or two, and departed from that car in quest of livelier society. Poor little gentleman! I suppose he thought an emigrant should be a rollicking, free-hearted blade, with a flask of foreign brandy and a long, comical story to beguile the moments of digestion.

Thursday.—I suppose there must be a cycle in the fatigue of travelling, for when I awoke next morning, I was entirely renewed in spirits and ate a hearty breakfast of porridge, with sweet milk, and coffee and hot cakes, at Burlington upon the Mississippi. Another long day's ride followed, with but one feature worthy of remark. At a place called Creston, a drunken man got in. He was aggressively friendly, but, according to English notions, not at all unpresentable upon a train. For one stage he eluded the notice of the officials; but just as we were beginning to move out of the next station, Cromwell by name, by came the conductor. There was a word or two of talk; and then the official had the man by the shoulders, twitched him from his seat, marched him through the car, and sent him flying on to the track. It was done in three motions, as exact as a piece of drill. The train was still moving slowly, although beginning to mend her pace, and the drunkard got his feet without a fall. He carried a red bundle, though not so red as his cheeks; and he shook this menacingly in the air with one hand, while the other stole behind him to the region of the kidneys. It was the first indication that I had come among revolvers, and I observed it with some emotion. The conductor stood on the steps with one hand on his hip, looking back at him; and perhaps this attitude imposed upon the creature, for he turned without further ado, and went off staggering along the track towards Cromwell, followed by a peal of laughter from the cars. They were speaking English all about me, but I knew I was in a foreign land.

Twenty minutes before nine that night, we were deposited at the Pacific Transfer Station near Council Bluffs, on the eastern bank of the Missouri river. Here we were to stay the night at a kind of caravanserai, set apart for emigrants. But I gave way to a thirst for luxury, separated myself from my companions, and marched with my effects into the Union Pacific Hotel. A white clerk and a coloured gentleman whom, in my plain European way, I should call the boots, were installed behind a counter like bank tellers. They took my name, assigned me a number, and proceeded to deal with my packages. And here came the tug of war. I wished to give up my packages into safe keeping; but I did not wish to go to bed. And this, it appeared, was impossible in an American hotel.

It was, of course, some inane misunderstanding, and sprang from my unfamiliarity with the language. For although two nations use the same words and read the same books, intercourse is not conducted by the dictionary. The business of life is not carried on by words, but in set phrases, each with a special and almost a slang signification. Some international obscurity prevailed between me and the coloured gentleman at Council Bluffs; so that what I was asking, which seemed very natural to me, appeared to him a monstrous exigency. He refused, and that with the plainness of the West. This American manner of conducting matters of business is, at first, highly unpalatable to the European. When we approach a man in the way of his calling, and for those services by which he earns his bread, we consider him for the time being our hired servant. But in the American opinion, two gentlemen meet and have a friendly talk with a view to exchanging favours if they shall agree to please. I know not which is the more convenient, nor even which is the more truly courteous. The English stiffness unfortunately tends to be continued after the particular transaction is at an end, and thus favours class separations. But on the other hand, these equalitarian plainnesses leave an open field for the insolence of Jack-in-office.

I was nettled by the coloured gentleman's refusal, and unbuttoned my wrath under the similitude of ironical submission. I knew nothing, I said, of the ways of American hotels; but I had no desire to give trouble. If there was nothing for it but to get to bed immediately, let him say the word, and though it was not my habit, I should cheerfully obey.

He burst into a shout of laughter. 'Ah!' said he, 'you do not know about America. They are fine people in America. Oh! you will like them very well. But you mustn't get mad. I know what you want. You come along with me.'

And issuing from behind the counter, and taking me by the arm like an old acquaintance, he led me to the bar of the hotel.

'There,' said he, pushing me from him by the shoulder, 'go and have a drink!'

THE EMIGRANT TRAIN

All this while I had been travelling by mixed trains, where I might meet with Dutch widows and little German gentry fresh from table. I had been but a latent emigrant; now I was to be branded once more, and put apart with my fellows. It was about two in the afternoon of Friday that I found myself in front of the Emigrant House, with more than a hundred others, to be sorted and boxed for the journey. A white-haired official, with a stick under one arm, and a list in the other hand, stood apart in front of us, and called name after name in the tone of a command. At each name you would see a family gather up its brats and bundles and run for the hindmost of the three cars that stood awaiting us, and I soon concluded that this was to be set apart for the women and children. The second or central car, it turned out, was devoted to men travelling alone, and the third to the Chinese. The official was easily moved to anger at the least delay ; but the emigrants were both quick at answering their names, and speedy in getting themselves and their effects on board.

The families once housed, we men carried the second car without ceremony by simultaneous assault. I suppose the reader has some notion of an American railroad-car, that long, narrow wooden box, like a flat-roofed Noah's ark, with a stove and a convenience, one at either end, a passage down the middle, and transverse benches upon either hand. Those destined for emigrants on the Union Pacific are only remarkable for their extreme plainness, nothing but wood entering in any part into their constitution, and for the usual inefficacy of the lamps, which often went out and shed but a dying glimmer even while they burned. The benches are too short for anything but a young child. Where there is scarce elbow-room for two to sit, there will not be space enough for one to lie. Hence the company, or rather, as

it appears from certain bills about the Transfer
Station, the company's servants, have conceived
a plan for the better accommodation of travellers.   They prevail on every two to chum
together.   To each of the chums they sell a
board and three square cushions stuffed with
straw, and covered with thin cotton.   The
benches can be made to face each other in
pairs, for the backs are reversible.   On the
approach of night the boards are laid from
bench to bench, making a couch wide enough
for two, and long enough for a man of the middle height; and the chums lie down side by side
upon the cushions with the head to the conductor's van and the feet to the engine.   When the
train is full, of course this plan is impossible,
for there must not be more than one to every
bench, neither can it be carried out unless the
chums agree.   It was to bring about this last
condition that our white-haired official now be-
stirred himself.   He made a most active master of ceremonies, introducing likely couples,
and even guaranteeing the amiability and
honesty of each.   The greater the number of
happy couples the better for his pocket, for it

was he who sold the raw material of the beds. His price for one board and three straw cushions began with two dollars and a half; but before the train left, and, I am sorry to say, long after I had purchased mine, it had fallen to one dollar and a half.

The match-maker had a difficulty with me; perhaps, like some ladies, I showed myself too eager for union at any price; but certainly the first who was picked out to be my bedfellow, declined the honour without thanks. He was an old, heavy, slow-spoken man, I think from Yankeeland, looked me all over with great timidity, and then began to excuse himself in broken phrases. He didn't know the young man, he said. The young man might be very honest, but how was he to know that? There was another young man whom he had met already in the train; he guessed *he* was honest, and would prefer to chum with *him* upon the whole. All this without any sort of excuse, as though I had been inanimate or absent. I began to tremble lest everyone should refuse my company, and I be left rejected. But the next in turn was a tall, strapping, long-limbed,

small-headed, curly-haired Pennsylvania Dutch-
man, with a soldierly smartness in his manner.
To be exact, he had acquired it in the navy.   But
that was all one; he had at least been trained
to desperate resolves, so he accepted the match,
and the white-haired swindler pronounced the
connubial benediction, and pocketed his fees.

The rest of the afternoon was spent in
making up the train.   I am afraid to say how
many baggage-waggons followed the engine,
certainly a score; then came the Chinese,
then we, then the families, and the rear was
brought up by the conductor in what, if I
have it rightly, is called his caboose.   The
class to which I belonged was of course far
the largest, and we ran over, so to speak, to
both sides; so that there were some Caucasians
among the Chinamen, and some bachelors
among the families.   But our own car was
pure from admixture, save for one little boy
of eight or nine, who had the whooping-
cough.   At last, about six, the long train
crawled out of the Transfer Station and
across the wide Missouri river to Omaha,
westward bound.

It was a troubled uncomfortable evening in the cars. There was thunder in the air, which helped to keep us restless. A man played many airs upon the cornet, and none of them were much attended to, until he came to 'Home, sweet home.' It was truly strange to note how the talk ceased at that, and the faces began to lengthen. I have no idea whether musically this air is to be considered good or bad; but it belongs to that class of art which may be best described as a brutal assault upon the feelings. Pathos must be relieved by dignity of treatment. If you wallow naked in the pathetic, like the author of 'Home, sweet home,' you make your hearers weep in an unmanly fashion; and even while yet they are moved, they despise themselves and hate the occasion of their weakness. It did not come to tears that night, for the experiment was interrupted. An elderly, hard-looking man, with a goatee beard and about as much appearance of sentiment as you would expect from a retired slaver, turned with a start and bade the performer stop that 'damned thing.' 'I've heard about enough of that,' he added; 'give us something about the good country we're going to.' A murmur of adhesion ran round the car; the performer took the instrument from his lips, laughed and nodded, and then struck into a dancing measure; and, like a new Timotheus, stilled immediately the emotion he had raised.

The day faded; the lamps were lit; a party of wild young men, who got off next evening at North Platte, stood together on the stern platform, singing 'The Sweet By-and-bye' with very tuneful voices; the chums began to put up their beds; and it seemed as if the business of the day were at an end. But it was not so; for, the train stopping at some station, the cars were instantly thronged with the natives, wives and fathers, young men and maidens, some of them in little more than nightgear, some with stable lanterns, and all offering beds for sale. Their charge began with twenty-five cents a cushion, but fell, before the train went on again, to fifteen, with the bed-board gratis, or less than one-fifth of what I had paid for mine at the Transfer. This is my contribution to the economy of future emigrants.

A great personage on an American train is the newsboy. He sells books (such books!), papers, fruit, lollipops, and cigars; and on emigrant journeys, soap, towels, tin washing dishes, tin coffee pitchers, coffee, tea, sugar, and tinned eatables, mostly hash or beans and bacon. Early next morning the newsboy went around the cars, and chumming on a more extended principle became the order of the hour. It requires but a copartnery of two to manage beds; but washing and eating can be carried on most economically by a syndicate of three. I myself entered a little after sunrise into articles of agreement, and became one of the firm of Pennsylvania, Shakespeare, and Dubuque. Shakespeare was my own nick-name on the cars; Pennsylvania that of my bedfellow; and Dubuque, the name of a place in the State of Iowa, that of an amiable young fellow going west to cure an asthma, and retarding his recovery by incessantly chewing or smoking, and sometimes chewing and smok-ing together. I have never seen tobacco so

sillily abused. Shakespeare bought a tin
washing-dish, Dubuque a towel, and Pennsylvania a brick of soap. The partners used
these instruments, one after another, according
to the order of their first awaking; and when
the firm had finished there was no want of
borrowers. Each filled the tin dish at the
water filter opposite the stove, and retired with
the whole stock in trade to the platform of the
car. There he knelt down, supporting himself
by a shoulder against the woodwork or one
elbow crooked about the railing, and made a
shift to wash his face and neck and hands; a
cold, an insufficient, and, if the train is moving
rapidly, a somewhat dangerous toilet.

On a similar division of expense, the firm
of Pennsylvania, Shakespeare, and Dubuque
supplied themselves with coffee, sugar, and
necessary vessels; and their operations are a
type of what went on through all the cars.
Before the sun was up the stove would be
brightly burning; at the first station the
natives would come on board with milk and
eggs and coffee cakes; and soon from end to
end the car would be filled with little parties

breakfasting upon the bed-boards. It was the pleasantest hour of the day.

There were meals to be had, however, by the wayside: a breakfast in the morning, a dinner somewhere between eleven and two, and supper from five to eight or nine at night. We had rarely less than twenty minutes for each; and if we had not spent many another twenty minutes waiting for some express upon a side track among miles of desert, we might have taken an hour to each repast and arrived at San Francisco up to time. For haste is not the foible of an emigrant train. It gets through on sufferance, running the gauntlet among its more considerable brethren; should there be a block, it is unhesitatingly sacrificed; and they cannot, in consequence, predict the length of the passage within a day or so. Civility is the main comfort that you miss. Equality, though conceived very largely in America, does not extend so low down as to an emigrant. Thus in all other trains, a warning cry of 'All aboard!' recalls the passengers to take their seats; but as soon as I was alone with emigrants, and from the Transfer all the way to San Francisco, I found this ceremony was pretermitted; the train stole from the station without note of warning, and you had to keep an eye upon it even while you ate. The annoyance is considerable, and the disrespect both wanton and petty.

Many conductors, again, will hold no communication with an emigrant. I asked a conductor one day at what time the train would stop for dinner; as he made no answer I repeated the question, with a like result; a third time I returned to the charge, and then Jack-in-office looked me coolly in the face for several seconds and turned ostentatiously away. I believe he was half ashamed of his brutality; for when another person made the same inquiry, although he still refused the information, he condescended to answer, and even to justify his reticence in a voice loud enough for me to hear. It was, he said, his principle not to tell people where they were to dine; for one answer led to many other questions, as what o'clock it was? or, how soon should we be there? and he could not afford to be eternally worried.

As you are thus cut off from the superior

authorities, a great deal of your comfort depends on the character of the newsboy. He has it in his power indefinitely to better and brighten the emigrant's lot. The newsboy with whom we started from the Transfer was a dark, bullying, contemptuous, insolent scoundrel, who treated us like dogs. Indeed, in his case, matters came nearly to a fight. It happened thus : he was going his rounds through the cars with some commodities for sale, and coming to a party who were at *Seven-up* or *Cascino* (our two games), upon a bed-board, slung down a cigar-box in the middle of the cards, knocking one man's hand to the floor. It was the last straw. In a moment the whole party were upon their feet, the cigars were upset, and he was ordered to 'get out of that directly, or he would get more than he reckoned for.' The fellow grumbled and muttered, but ended by making off, and was less openly insulting in the future. On the other hand, the lad who rode with us in this capacity from Ogden to Sacramento made himself the friend of all, and helped us with information, attention, assistance, and a kind countenance. He told us where and when we should have our meals, and how long the train would stop; kept seats at table for those who were delayed, and watched that we should neither be left behind nor yet unnecessarily hurried. You, who live at home at ease, can hardly realise the greatness of this service, even had it stood alone. When I think of that lad coming and going, train after train, with his bright face and civil words, I see how easily a good man may become the benefactor of his kind. Perhaps he is discontented with himself, perhaps troubled with ambitions; why, if he but knew it, he is a hero of the old Greek stamp; and while he thinks he is only earning a profit of a few cents, and that perhaps exorbitant, he is doing a man's work, and bettering the world.

I must tell here an experience of mine with another newsboy. I tell it because it gives so good an example of that uncivil kindness of the American, which is perhaps their most bewildering character to one newly landed. It was immediately after I had left the emigrant train; and I am told I looked like a man at death's door, so much had this long journey shaken me.

I sat at the end of a car, and the catch being broken, and myself feverish and sick, I had to hold the door open with my foot for the sake of air. In this attitude my leg debarred the newsboy from his box of merchandise. I made haste to let him pass when I observed that he was coming; but I was busy with a book, and so once or twice he came upon me unawares. On these occasions he most rudely struck my foot aside; and though I myself apologised, as if to show him the way, he answered me never a word. I chafed furiously, and I fear the next time it would have come to words. But suddenly I felt a touch upon my shoulder, and a large juicy pear was put into my hand. It was the newsboy, who had observed that I was looking ill and so made me this present out of a tender heart. For the rest of the journey I was petted like a sick child; he lent me newspapers, thus depriving himself of his legitimate profit on their sale, and came repeatedly to sit by me and cheer me up.

THE PLAINS OF NEBRASKA

It had thundered on the Friday night, but the sun rose on Saturday without a cloud. We were at sea—there is no other adequate expression—on the plains of Nebraska. I made my observatory on the top of a fruit-waggon, and sat by the hour upon that perch to spy about me, and to spy in vain for something new. It was a world almost without a feature; an empty sky, an empty earth; front and back, the line of railway stretched from horizon to horizon, like a cue across a billiard-board; on either hand, the green plain ran till it touched the skirts of heaven. Along the track innumerable wild sunflowers, no bigger than a crown-piece, bloomed in a continuous flower-bed; grazing beasts were seen upon the prairie at all degrees of distance and diminution; and now and again we might perceive a few dots beside the railroad which grew more and more distinct as we drew nearer till they turned into wooden cabins, and then dwindled and dwindled in our wake until they melted into their surroundings, and we were once more alone upon the billiard-board. The train toiled over this infinity like a snail; and being the one thing moving, it was wonderful what huge proportions it began to assume in our regard. It seemed miles in length, and either end of it within but a step of the horizon. Even my own body or my own head seemed a great thing in that emptiness. I note the feeling the more readily as it is the contrary of what I have read of in the experience of others. Day and night, above the roar of the train, our ears were kept busy with the incessant chirp of grasshoppers—a noise like the winding up of countless clocks and watches, which began after a while to seem proper to that land.

To one hurrying through by steam there was a certain exhilaration in this spacious vacancy, this greatness of the air, this discovery of the whole arch of heaven, this straight, unbroken, prison-line of the horizon. Yet one could not but reflect upon the weariness of those who passed by there in old days, at the foot's pace of oxen, painfully urging their teams, and with no landmark but that unattainable evening sun for which they steered, and which daily fled

them by an equal stride. They had nothing, it
would seem, to overtake; nothing by which
to reckon their advance; no sight for repose or
for encouragement; but stage after stage, only
the dead green waste under foot, and the mock-
ing, fugitive horizon. But the eye, as I have
been told, found differences even here; and at
the worst the emigrant came, by perseverance,
to the end of his toil. It is the settlers, after
all, at whom we have a right to marvel. Our
consciousness, by which we live, is itself but the
creature of variety. Upon what food does it
subsist in such a land? What livelihood can
repay a human creature for a life spent in this
huge sameness? He is cut off from books,
from news, from company, from all that can
relieve existence but the prosecution of his
affairs. A sky full of stars is the most varied
spectacle that he can hope. He may walk five
miles and see nothing; ten, and it is as though
he had not moved; twenty, and still he is in
the midst of the same great level, and has
approached no nearer to the one object within
view, the flat horizon which keeps pace with his
advance. We are full at home of the question

of agreeable wall-papers, and wise people are of
opinion that the temper may be quieted by
sedative surroundings. But what is to be said
of the Nebraskan settler? His is a wall-paper
with a vengeance—one quarter of the universe
laid bare in all its gauntness. His eye must
embrace at every glance the whole seeming
concave of the visible world; it quails before so
vast an outlook, it is tortured by distance; yet
there is no rest or shelter, till the man runs into
his cabin, and can repose his sight upon things
near at hand. Hence, I am told, a sickness of
the vision peculiar to these empty plains.

Yet perhaps with sunflowers and cicadæ,
summer and winter, cattle, wife and family,
the settler may create a full and various existence. One person at least I saw upon the
plains who seemed in every way superior to
her lot. This was a woman who boarded us
at a way station, selling milk. She was largely
formed; her features were more than comely;
she had that great rarity—a fine complexion
which became her; and her eyes were kind,
dark, and steady. She sold milk with patri-
archal grace. There was not a line in her

countenance, not a note in her soft and sleepy voice, but spoke of an entire contentment with her life. It would have been fatuous arrogance to pity such a woman. Yet the place where she lived was to me almost ghastly. Less than a dozen wooden houses, all of a shape and all nearly of a size, stood planted along the railway lines. Each stood apart in its own lot. Each opened direct off the billiard-board, as if it were a billiard-board indeed, and these only models that had been set down upon it ready made. Her own, into which I looked, was clean but very empty, and showed nothing homelike but the burning fire. This extreme newness, above all in so naked and flat a country, gives a strong impression of artificiality. With none of the litter and discoloration of human life; with the paths unworn, and the houses still sweating from the axe, such a settlement as this seems purely scenic. The mind is loth to accept it for a piece of reality; and it seems incredible that life can go on with so few properties, or the great child, man, find entertainment in so bare a playroom.

And truly it is as yet an incomplete society

in some points; or at least it contained, as I passed through, one person incompletely civilised. At North Platte, where we supped that evening, one man asked another to pass the milk-jug. This other was well-dressed and of what we should call a respectable appearance; a darkish man, high spoken, eating as though he had some usage of society; but he turned upon the first speaker with extraordinary vehemence of tone—

'There's a waiter here!' he cried.

'I only asked you to pass the milk,' explained the first.

Here is the retort verbatim—

'Pass! Hell! I'm not paid for that business; the waiter's paid for it. You should use civility at table, and, by God, I'll show you how!'

The other man very wisely made no answer, and the bully went on with his supper as though nothing had occurred. It pleases me to think that some day soon he will meet with one of his own kidney; and that perhaps both may fall.

THE DESERT OF WYOMING

To cross such a plain is to grow homesick for the mountains. I longed for the Black Hills of Wyoming, which I knew we were soon to enter, like an ice-bound whaler for the spring. Alas! and it was a worse country than the other. All Sunday and Monday we travelled through these sad mountains, or over the main ridge of the Rockies, which is a fair match to them for misery of aspect. Hour after hour it was the same unhomely and unkindly world about our onward path; tumbled boulders, cliffs that drearily imitate the shape of monuments and fortifications—how drearily, how tamely, none can tell who has not seen them; not a tree, not a patch of sward, not one shapely or commanding mountain form; sage-brush, eternal sage-brush; over all, the same weariful and gloomy colouring, grays warming into brown, grays darkening towards black; and for sole sign of life, here and there a few fleeing antelopes; here and there, but at incredible intervals, a creek running in a cañon. The plains have a grandeur of their own; but here there is nothing but a contorted smallness. Except for the air, which was light and stimulating, there was not one good circumstance in that God-forsaken land.

I had been suffering in my health a good deal all the way; and at last, whether I was exhausted by my complaint or poisoned in some wayside eating-house, the evening we left Laramie, I fell sick outright. That was a night which I shall not readily forget. The lamps did not go out; each made a faint shining in its own neighbourhood, and the shadows were confounded together in the long, hollow box of the car. The sleepers lay in uneasy attitudes; here two chums alongside, flat upon their backs like dead folk; there a man sprawling on the floor, with his face upon his arm; there another half seated with his head and shoulders on the bench. The most passive were continually and roughly shaken by the movement of the train; others stirred, turned, or stretched out their arms like children; it was surprising how many groaned and murmured in their sleep; and as I passed to and fro, stepping across the

prostrate, and caught now a snore, now a gasp,
now a half-formed word, it gave me a measure
of the worthlessness of rest in that unresting
vehicle. Although it was chill, I was obliged
to open my window, for the degradation of the
air soon became intolerable to one who was
awake and using the full supply of life. Outside, in a glimmering night, I saw the black,
amorphous hills shoot by unweariedly into our
wake. They that long for morning have never
longed for it more earnestly than I.

And yet when day came, it was to shine
upon the same broken and unsightly quarter of
the world. Mile upon mile, and not a tree, a
bird, or a river. Only down the long, sterile
cañons, the train shot hooting and awoke the
resting echo. That train was the one piece of
life in all the deadly land; it was the one
actor, the one spectacle fit to be observed in
this paralysis of man and nature. And when
I think how the railroad has been pushed
through this unwatered wilderness and haunt
of savage tribes, and now will bear an emigrant
for some £12 from the Atlantic to the Golden
Gates; how at each stage of the construction,

roaring, impromptu cities, full of gold and lust and death, sprang up and then died away again, and are now but wayside stations in the desert; how in these uncouth places pig-tailed Chinese pirates worked side by side with border ruffians and broken men from Europe, talking together in a mixed dialect, mostly oaths, gambling, drinking, quarrelling and murdering like wolves; how the plumed hereditary lord of all America heard, in this last fastness, the scream of the 'bad medicine waggon' charioting his foes; and then when I go on to remember that all this epical turmoil was conducted by gentlemen in frock coats, and with a view to nothing more extraordinary than a fortune and a subsequent visit to Paris, it seems to me, I own, as if this railway were the one typical achievement of the age in which we live, as if it brought together into one plot all the ends of the world and all the degrees of social rank, and offered to some great writer the busiest, the most extended, and the most varied subject for an enduring literary work. If it be romance, if it be contrast, if it be heroism that we require, what was Troy town to this? But, alas! it is not these things that are necessary—it is only Homer.

Here also we are grateful to the train, as to some god who conducts us swiftly through these shades and by so many hidden perils. Thirst, hunger, the sleight and ferocity of Indians are all no more feared, so lightly do we skim these horrible lands; as the gull, who wings safely through the hurricane and past the shark. Yet we should not be forgetful of these hardships of the past; and to keep the balance true, since I have complained of the trifling discomforts of my journey, perhaps more than was enough, let me add an original document. It was not written by Homer, but by a boy of eleven, long since dead, and is dated only twenty years ago. I shall punctuate, to make things clearer, but not change the spelling.

'*My dear Sister Mary,*—*I am afraid you will go nearly crazy when you read my letter. If Jerry*' (*the writer's eldest brother*) '*has not written to you before now, you will be surprised to heare that we are in California, and that poor Thomas*' (*another brother, of fifteen*)

'*is dead. We started from* ———— *in July,
with plenty of provisions and too yoke oxen. We
went along very well till we got within six or
seven hundred miles of California, when the
Indians attacked us. We found places where
they had killed the emigrants. We had one
passenger with us, too guns, and one revolver;
so we ran all the lead We had into bullets (and)
hung the guns up in the wagon so that we could
get at them in a minit. It was about two o'clock
in the afternoon; droave the cattel a little way;
when a prairie chicken alited a little way from
the wagon.*

'*Jerry took out one of the guns to shoot it,
and told Tom drive the oxen. Tom and I
drove the oxen, and Jerry and the passenger went
on. Then, after a little, I left Tom and caught
up with Jerry and the other man. Jerry stopped
for Tom to come up; me and the man went on
and sit down by a little stream. In a few
minutes, we heard some noise; then three shots
(they all struck poor Tom, I suppose); then they
gave the war hoop, and as many as twenty of the
red skins came down upon us. The three that shot
Tom was hid by the side of the road in the bushes.*

'*I thought the Tom and Jerry were shot; so
I told the other man that Tom and Jerry were
dead, and that we had better try to escape, if
possible. I had no shoes on; having a sore foot,
I thought I would not put them on. The man
and me run down the road, but We was soon
stopt by an Indian on a pony. We then turend
the other way, and run up the side of the Mountain, and hid behind some cedar trees, and stayed
there till dark. The Indians hunted all over
after us, and verry close to us, so close that we
could here there tomyhawks Jingle. At dark the
man and me started on, I stubing my toes against
sticks and stones. We traveld on all night;
and next morning, Just as it was getting gray, we
saw something in the shape of a man. It layed
Down in the grass. We went up to it, and it
was Jerry. He thought we ware Indians. You
can imagine how glad he was to see me. He
thought we was all dead but him, and we thought
him and Tom was dead. He had the gun that
he took out of the wagon to shoot the prairie
Chicken; all he had was the load that was in it.*

'*We traveld on till about eight o'clock, We
caught up with one wagon with too men with it.*

We had traveld with them before one day; we stopt and they Drove on; we knew that they was ahead of us, unless they had been killed to. My feet was so sore when we caught up with them that I had to ride; I could not step. We traveld on for too days, when the men that owned the cattle said they would (could) not drive them another inch. We unyoked the oxen; we had about seventy pounds of flour; we took it out and divided it into four packs. Each of the men took about 18 pounds apiece and a blanket. I carried a little bacon, dried meat, and little quilt; I had in all about twelve pounds. We had one pint of flour a day for our alloyance. Sometimes we made soup of it; sometimes we (made) pancakes; and sometimes mixed it up with cold water and eat it that way. We traveld twelve or fourteen days. The time came at last when we should have to reach some place or starve. We saw fresh horse and cattle tracks. The morning come, we scraped all the flour out of the sack, mixed it up, and baked it into bread, and made some soup, and eat everything we had. We traveld on all day without anything to eat, and that evening we Caught up with a sheep train of eight wagons. We traveld with them till we arrived at the settlements; and know I am safe in California, and got to good home, and going to school.

'*Jerry is working in* ————. *It is a good country. You can get from* 50 *to* 60 *and* 75 *Dollars for cooking. Tell me all about the affairs in the States, and how all the folks get along.*'

And so ends this artless narrative. The little man was at school again, God bless him, while his brother lay scalped upon the deserts.

FELLOW PASSENGERS

At Ogden we changed cars from the Union Pacific to the Central Pacific line of railroad. The change was doubly welcome; for, first, we had better cars on the new line; and, second, those in which we had been cooped for more than ninety hours had begun to stink abominably. Several yards away, as we returned, let us say from dinner, our nostrils were assailed by rancid air. I have stood on a platform while the whole train was shunting; and as the

dwelling-cars drew near, there would come a
whiff of pure menagerie, only a little sourer, as
from men instead of monkeys. I think we are
human only in virtue of open windows. Without fresh air, you only require a bad heart, and
a remarkable command of the Queen's English,
to become such another as Dean Swift; a kind
of leering, human goat, leaping and wagging
your scut on mountains of offence. I do my
best to keep my head the other way, and look
for the human rather than the bestial in this
Yahoo-like business of the emigrant train. But
one thing I must say, the car of the Chinese
was notably the least offensive.

The cars on the Central Pacific were nearly
twice as high, and so proportionally airier;
they were freshly varnished, which gave us all
a sense of cleanliness as though we had bathed;
the seats drew out and joined in the centre, so
that there was no more need for bed boards;
and there was an upper tier of berths which
could be closed by day and opened at night.

I had by this time some opportunity of
seeing the people whom I was among. They
were in rather marked contrast to the emi-

grants I had met on board ship while crossing the Atlantic. They were mostly lumpish fellows, silent and noisy, a common combination; somewhat sad, I should say, with an extraordinary poor taste in humour, and little interest in their fellow-creatures beyond that of a cheap and merely external curiosity. If they heard a man's name and business, they seemed to think they had the heart of that mystery; but they were as eager to know that much as they were indifferent to the rest. Some of them were on nettles till they learned your name was Dickson and you a journeyman baker; but beyond that, whether you were Catholic or Mormon, dull or clever, fierce or friendly, was all one to them. Others who were not so stupid, gossiped a little, and, I am bound to say, unkindly. A favourite witticism was for some lout to raise the alarm of 'All aboard!' while the rest of us were dining, thus contributing his mite to the general discomfort. Such a one was always much applauded for his high spirits. When I was ill coming through Wyoming, I was astonished—fresh from the eager humanity on board ship—to meet with little but laughter. One of the young men even amused himself by incommoding me, as was then very easy; and that not from ill-nature, but mere clodlike incapacity to think, for he expected me to join the laugh. I did so, but it was phantom merriment. Later on, a man from Kansas had three violent epileptic fits, and though, of course, there were not wanting some to help him, it was rather superstitious terror than sympathy that his case evoked among his fellow-passengers. 'Oh, I hope he's not going to die!' cried a woman; 'it would be terrible to have a dead body!' And there was a very general movement to leave the man behind at the next station. This, by good fortune, the conductor negatived.

There was a good deal of story-telling in some quarters; in others, little but silence. In this society, more than any other that ever I was in, it was the narrator alone who seemed to enjoy the narrative. It was rarely that any one listened for the listening. If he lent an ear to another man's story, it was because he was in immediate want of a hearer for one of his own. Food and the progress of the train were the subjects most generally treated; many joined to discuss these who otherwise would hold their tongues.   One small knot had no better occupation than to worm out of me my name; and the more they tried, the more obstinately fixed I grew to baffle them.   They assailed me with artful questions and insidious offers of correspondence in the future; but I was perpetually on my guard, and parried their assaults with inward laughter.   I am sure Dubuque would have given me ten dollars for the secret.   He owed me far more, had he understood life, for thus preserving him a lively interest throughout the journey.   I met one of my fellow-passengers months after, driving a street tramway car in San Francisco; and, as the joke was now out of season, told him my name without subterfuge.   You never saw a man more chapfallen.   But had my name been Demogorgon, after so prolonged a mystery he had still been disappointed.

There were no emigrants direct from Europe—save one German family and a knot of Cornish miners who kept grimly by themselves, one reading the New Testament all day long through steel spectacles, the rest discussing privately the secrets of their old-world, mysterious race. Lady Hester Stanhope believed she could make something great of the Cornish; for my part, I can make nothing of them at all. A division of races, older and more original than that of Babel, keeps this close, esoteric family apart from neighbouring Englishmen. Not even a Red Indian seems more foreign in my eyes. This is one of the lessons of travel—that some of the strangest races dwell next door to you at home.

The rest were all American born, but they came from almost every quarter of that Continent. All the States of the North had sent out a fugitive to cross the plains with me. From Virginia, from Pennsylvania, from New York, from far western Iowa and Kansas, from Maine that borders on the Canadas, and from the Canadas themselves—some one or two were fleeing in quest of a better land and better wages. The talk in the train, like the talk I heard on the steamer, ran upon hard times, short commons, and hope that moves ever westward. I thought of my shipful from Great

Britain with a feeling of despair. They had
come 3000 miles, and yet not far enough.
Hard times bowed them out of the Clyde, and
stood to welcome them at Sandy Hook.
Where were they to go? Pennsylvania, Maine,
Iowa, Kansas? These were not places for
immigration, but for emigration, it appeared;
not one of them, but I knew a man who had
lifted up his heel and left it for an ungrate-
ful country. And it was still westward that
they ran. Hunger, you would have thought,
came out of the east like the sun, and the
evening was made of edible gold. And, meantime, in the car in front of me, were there not
half a hundred emigrants from the opposite
quarter? Hungry Europe and hungry China,
each pouring from their gates in search of prov-
ender, had here come face to face. The two
waves had met; east and west had alike failed;
the whole round world had been prospected
and condemned; there was no El Dorado
anywhere; and till one could emigrate to the
moon, it seemed as well to stay patiently
at home. Nor was there wanting another sign,
at once more picturesque and more dishearten-

ing; for, as we continued to steam westward toward the land of gold, we were continually passing other emigrant trains upon the journey east; and these were as crowded as our own. Had all these return voyagers made a fortune in the mines? Were they all bound for Paris, and to be in Rome by Easter? It would seem not, for, whenever we met them, the passengers ran on the platform and cried to us through the windows, in a kind of wailing chorus, to 'Come back.' On the plains of Nebraska, in the mountains of Wyoming, it was still the same cry, and dismal to my heart, 'Come back!' That was what we heard by the way 'about the good country we were going to.' And at that very hour the Sand-lot of San Francisco was crowded with the unemployed, and the echo from the other side of Market Street was repeating the rant of demagogues.

If, in truth, it were only for the sake of wages that men emigrate, how many thousands would regret the bargain! But wages, indeed, are only one consideration out of many; for we are a race of gipsies, and love change and travel for themselves.

DESPISED RACES

Of all stupid ill-feelings, the sentiment of my fellow-Caucasians towards our companions in the Chinese car was the most stupid and the worst. They seemed never to have looked at them, listened to them, or thought of them, but hated them *a priori*. The Mongols were their enemies in that cruel and treacherous battle-field of money. They could work better and cheaper in half a hundred industries, and hence there was no calumny too idle for the Caucasians to repeat, and even to believe. They declared them hideous vermin, and affected a kind of choking in the throat when they beheld them. Now, as a matter of fact, the young Chinese man is so like a large class of European women, that on raising my head and suddenly catching sight of one at a considerable distance, I have for an instant been deceived by the resemblance. I do not say it is the most attractive class of our women, but for all that many a man's wife is less pleasantly favoured. Again, my emigrants declared that the Chinese were dirty. I cannot say they were clean, for that was impossible upon the journey; but in their efforts after cleanliness they put the rest of us to shame. We all pigged and stewed in one infamy, wet our hands and faces for half a minute daily on the platform, and were unashamed. But the Chinese never lost an opportunity, and you would see them washing their feet—an act not dreamed of among ourselves—and going as far as decency permitted to wash their whole bodies. I may remark by the way that the dirtier people are in their persons the more delicate is their sense of modesty. A clean man strips in a crowded boathouse; but he who is unwashed slinks in and out of bed without uncovering an inch of skin. Lastly, these very foul and mal-odorous Caucasians entertained the surprising illusion that it was the Chinese waggon, and that alone, which stank. I have said already that it was the exception, and notably the freshest of the three.

These judgments are typical of the feeling in all Western America. The Chinese are considered stupid, because they are imperfectly acquainted with English. They are held to be base, because their dexterity and frugality en-

able them to underbid the lazy, luxurious
Caucasian. They are said to be thieves; I am
sure they have no monopoly of that. They
are called cruel; the Anglo-Saxon and the
cheerful Irishman may each reflect before he
bears the accusation. I am told, again, that
they are of the race of river pirates, and belong
to the most despised and dangerous class in the
Celestial Empire. But if this be so, what
remarkable pirates have we here! and what
must be the virtues, the industry, the education,
and the intelligence of their superiors at home!

Awhile ago it was the Irish, now it is the
Chinese that must go. Such is the cry. It
seems, after all, that no country is bound to
submit to immigration any more than to
invasion: each is war to the knife, and resist-
ance to either but legitimate defence. Yet we
may regret the free tradition of the republic,
which loved to depict herself with open arms,
welcoming all unfortunates. And certainly, as
a man who believes that he loves freedom, I
may be excused some bitterness when I find
her sacred name misused in the contention. It
was but the other day that I heard a vulgar

fellow in the Sand-lot, the popular tribune of San Francisco, roaring for arms and butchery. 'At the call of Abreham Lincoln,' said the orator, 'ye rose in the name of freedom to set free the negroes; can ye not rise and liberate yourselves from a few dhirty Mongolians?'

For my own part, I could not look but with wonder and respect on the Chinese. Their forefathers watched the stars before mine had begun to keep pigs. Gunpowder and printing, which the other day we imitated, and a school of manners which we never had the delicacy so much as to desire to imitate, were theirs in a long-past antiquity. They walk the earth with us, but it seems they must be of different clay. They hear the clock strike the same hour, yet surely of a different epoch. They travel by steam conveyance, yet with such a baggage of old Asiatic thoughts and superstitions as might check the locomotive in its course. Whatever is thought within the circuit of the Great Wall; what the wry-eyed, spectacled schoolmaster teaches in the hamlets round Pekin; religions so old that our language looks a halfling boy alongside; philosophy so wise that our best

philosophers find things therein to wonder at;
all this travelled alongside of me for thousands
of miles over plain and mountain.   Heaven
knows if we had one common thought or fancy
all that way, or whether our eyes, which yet
were formed upon the same design, beheld the
same world out of the railway windows.   And
when either of us turned his thoughts to home
and childhood, what a strange dissimilarity must
there not have been in these pictures of the
mind—when I beheld that old, gray, castled
city, high throned above the firth, with the flag
of Britain flying, and the red-coat sentry pacing
over all; and the man in the next car to me
would conjure up some junks and a pagoda and
a fort of porcelain, and call it, with the same
affection, home.

Another race shared among my fellow-
passengers in the disfavour of the Chinese; and
that, it is hardly necessary to say, was the noble
red man of old story—he over whose own
hereditary continent we had been steaming all
these days.   I saw no wild or independent
Indian; indeed, I hear that such avoid the
neighbourhood of the train; but now and again

at way stations, a husband and wife and a few children, disgracefully dressed out with the sweepings of civilisation, came forth and stared upon the emigrants. The silent stoicism of their conduct, and the pathetic degradation of their appearance, would have touched any thinking creature, but my fellow-passengers danced and jested round them with a truly Cockney baseness. I was ashamed for the thing we call civilisation. We should carry upon our consciences so much, at least, of our forefathers' misconduct as we continue to profit by ourselves.

If oppression drives a wise man mad, what should be raging in the hearts of these poor tribes, who have been driven back and back, step after step, their promised reservations torn from them one after another as the States extended westward, until at length they are shut up into these hideous mountain deserts of the centre— and even there find themselves invaded, insulted, and hunted out by ruffianly diggers? The eviction of the Cherokees (to name but an instance), the extortion of Indian agents, the outrages of the wicked, the ill-faith of all, nay,

down to the ridicule of such poor beings as were
here with me upon the train, make up a chapter of injustice and indignity such as a man
must be in some ways base if his heart will
suffer him to pardon or forget. These old,
well-founded, historical hatreds have a savour
of nobility for the independent. That the Jew
should not love the Christian, nor the Irishman
love the English, nor the Indian brave tolerate
the thought of the American, is not disgraceful
to the nature of man; rather, indeed, honour-
able, since it depends on wrongs ancient like
the race, and not personal to him who cherishes
the indignation.

TO THE GOLDEN GATES

A little corner of Utah is soon traversed,
and leaves no particular impressions on the
mind. By an early hour on Wednesday morning we stopped to breakfast at Toano, a little
station on a bleak, high-lying plateau in Ne-
vada. The man who kept the station eating-
house was a Scot, and learning that I was
the same, he grew very friendly, and gave me

some advice on the country I was now entering. 'You see,' said he, 'I tell you this, because I come from your country.' Hail, brither Scots!

His most important hint was on the moneys of this part of the world. There is something in the simplicity of a decimal coinage which is revolting to the human mind; thus the French, in small affairs, reckon strictly by halfpence; and you have to solve, by a spasm of mental arithmetic, such posers as thirty-two, forty-five, or even a hundred halfpence. In the Pacific States they have made a bolder push for complexity, and settle their affairs by a coin that no longer exists—the *bit*, or old Mexican real. The supposed value of the bit is twelve and a half cents, eight to the dollar. When it comes to two bits, the quarter-dollar stands for the required amount. But how about an odd bit? The nearest coin to it is a dime, which is short by a fifth. That, then, is called a *short bit*. If you have one, you lay it triumphantly down, and save two and a half cents. But if you have not, and lay down a quarter, the bar-keeper or shopman calmly tenders you a dime by way of change; and thus you have paid what is called a *long bit*, and lost two and a half cents, or even, by comparison with a short bit, five cents. In country places all over the Pacific coast, nothing lower than a bit is ever asked or taken, which vastly increases the cost of life; as even for a glass of beer you must pay fivepence or sevenpence-halfpenny, as the case may be. You would say that this system of mutual robbery was as broad as it was long; but I have discovered a plan to make it broader, with which I here endow the public. It is brief and simple—radiantly simple. There is one place where five cents are recognised, and that is the post-office. A quarter is only worth two bits, a short and a long. Whenever you have a quarter, go to the post-office and buy five cents' worth of postage-stamps; you will receive in change two dimes, that is, two short bits. The purchasing power of your money is undiminished. You can go and have your two glasses of beer all the same; and you have made yourself a present of five cents' worth of postage-stamps into the bargain. Benjamin Franklin would have patted me on the head for this discovery.

From Toano we travelled all day through deserts of alkali and sand, horrible to man, and bare sage-brush country that seemed little kindlier, and came by supper-time to Elko. As we were standing, after our manner, outside the station, I saw two men whip suddenly from underneath the cars, and take to their heels across country. They were tramps, it appeared, who had been riding on the beams since eleven of the night before; and several of my fellow-passengers had already seen and conversed with them while we broke our fast at Toano. These land stowaways play a great part over here in America, and I should have liked dearly to become acquainted with them.

At Elko an odd circumstance befell me. I was coming out from supper, when I was stopped by a small, stout, ruddy man, followed by two others taller and ruddier than himself.

' Ex-cuse me, sir,' he said, ' but do you happen to be going on ? '

I said I was, whereupon he said he hoped to persuade me to desist from that intention. He had a situation to offer me, and if we could come to terms, why, good and well. 'You see,' he continued, 'I'm running a theatre here, and we're a little short in the orchestra. You're a musician, I guess?'

I assured him that, beyond a rudimentary acquaintance with 'Auld Lang Syne' and 'The Wearing of the Green,' I had no pretension whatever to that style. He seemed much put out of countenance; and one of his taller companions asked him, on the nail, for five dollars.

'You see, sir,' added the latter to me, 'he bet you were a musician; I bet you weren't. No offence, I hope?'

'None whatever,' I said, and the two withdrew to the bar, where I presume the debt was liquidated.

This little adventure woke bright hopes in my fellow-travellers, who thought they had now come to a country where situations went a-begging. But I am not so sure that the offer was in good faith. Indeed, I am more than half persuaded it was but a feeler to decide the bet.

Of all the next day I will tell you nothing,

for the best of all reasons, that I remember no
more than that we continued through desolate
and desert scenes, fiery hot and deadly weary.
But some time after I had fallen asleep that
night, I was awakened by one of my companions. It was in vain that I resisted. A
fire of enthusiasm and whisky burned in his
eyes; and he declared we were in a new
country, and I must come forth upon the platform and see with my own eyes. The train
was then, in its patient way, standing halted in
a by-track. It was a clear, moonlit night;
but the valley was too narrow to admit the
moonshine direct, and only a diffused glimmer
whitened the tall rocks and relieved the blackness of the pines. A hoarse clamour filled the
air; it was the continuous plunge of a cascade
somewhere near at hand among the mountains.
The air struck chill, but tasted good and vigorous in the nostrils—a fine, dry, old mountain
atmosphere. I was dead sleepy, but I returned
to roost with a grateful mountain feeling at my
heart.

When I awoke next morning, I was puzzled
for a while to know if it were day or night,

for the illumination was unusual. I sat up at last, and found we were grading slowly downward through a long snowshed; and suddenly we shot into an open; and before we were swallowed into the next length of wooden tunnel, I had one glimpse of a huge pine-forested ravine upon my left, a foaming river, and a sky already coloured with the fires of dawn. I am usually very calm over the displays of nature; but you will scarce believe how my heart leaped at this. It was like meeting one's wife. I had come home again —home from unsightly deserts to the green and habitable corners of the earth. Every spire of pine along the hill-top, every trouty pool along that mountain river, was more dear to me than a blood relation. Few people have praised God more happily than I did. And thenceforward, down by Blue Cañon, Alta, Dutch Flat, and all the old mining camps, through a sea of mountain forests, dropping thousands of feet toward the far sea-level as we went, not I only, but all the passengers on board, threw off their sense of dirt and heat and weariness, and bawled like schoolboys, and thronged with shining eyes upon the platform and became new creatures within and without. The sun no longer oppressed us with heat, it only shone laughingly along the mountain-side, until we were fain to laugh ourselves for glee. At every turn we could see farther into the land and our own happy futures. At every town the cocks were tossing their clear notes into the golden air, and crowing for the new day and the new country. For this was indeed our destination; this was 'the good country' we had been going to so long.

By afternoon we were at Sacramento, the city of gardens in a plain of corn; and the next day before the dawn we were lying to upon the Oakland side of San Francisco Bay. The day was breaking as we crossed the ferry; the fog was rising over the citied hills of San Francisco; the bay was perfect— not a ripple, scarce a stain, upon its blue expanse; everything was waiting, breathless, for the sun. A spot of cloudy gold lit first upon the head of Tamalpais, and then widened downward on its shapely shoulder; the air seemed to awaken, and began to sparkle; and suddenly

> 'The tall hills Titan discovered,'

and the city of San Francisco, and the bay of gold and corn, were lit from end to end with summer daylight.

[1879.]

II

THE OLD PACIFIC CAPITAL:

THE WOODS AND THE PACIFIC

THE Bay of Monterey has been compared by
no less a person than General Sherman to
a bent fishing-hook; and the comparison, if
less important than the march through Georgia,
still shows the eye of a soldier for topography.
Santa Cruz sits exposed at the shank; the
mouth of the Salinas river is at the middle
of the bend; and Monterey itself is cosily
ensconced beside the barb. Thus the ancient
capital of California faces across the bay, while
the Pacific Ocean, though hidden by low hills
and forest, bombards her left flank and rear
with never-dying surf. In front of the town,
the long line of sea-beach trends north and
north-west, and then westward to enclose the

bay. The waves which lap so quietly about the jetties of Monterey grow louder and larger in the distance; you can see the breakers leaping high and white by day; at night, the outline of the shore is traced in transparent silver by the moonlight and the flying foam; and from all round, even in quiet weather, the low, distant, thrilling roar of the Pacific hangs over the coast and the adjacent country like smoke above a battle.

These long beaches are enticing to the idle man. It would be hard to find a walk more solitary and at the same time more exciting to the mind. Crowds of ducks and sea-gulls hover over the sea. Sandpipers trot in and out by troops after the retiring waves, trilling together in a chorus of infinitesimal song. Strange sea-tangles, new to the European eye, the bones of whales, or sometimes a whole whale's carcase, white with carrion-gulls and poisoning the wind, lie scattered here and there along the sands. The waves come in slowly, vast and green, curve their translucent necks, and burst with a surprising uproar, that runs, waxing and waning, up and down the

long key-board of the beach. The foam of
these great ruins mounts in an instant to the
ridge of the sand glacis, swiftly fleets back
again, and is met and buried by the next
breaker. The interest is perpetually fresh.
On no other coast that I know shall you enjoy,
in calm, sunny weather, such a spectacle of
Ocean's greatness, such beauty of changing
colour, or such degrees of thunder in the sound.
The very air is more than usually salt by this
Homeric deep.

Inshore, a tract of sand-hills borders on the
beach. Here and there a lagoon, more or less
brackish, attracts the birds and hunters. A
rough, spotty undergrowth partially conceals
the sand. The crouching, hardy, live-oaks
flourish singly or in thickets—the kind of wood
for murderers to crawl among—and here and
there the skirts of the forest extend downward
from the hills with a floor of turf and long
aisles of pine-trees hung with Spaniard's
Beard. Through this quaint desert the railway
cars drew near to Monterey from the junction
at Salinas City—though that and so many
other things are now for ever altered—and it

was from here that you had the first view of the
old township lying in the sands, its white
windmills bickering in the chill, perpetual wind,
and the first fogs of the evening drawing
drearily around it from the sea.

The one common note of all this country is
the haunting presence of the ocean. A great
faint sound of breakers follows you high up
into the inland cañons; the roar of water
dwells in the clean, empty rooms of Monterey
as in a shell upon the chimney; go where you
will you have but to pause and listen to hear
the voice of the Pacific. You pass out of the
town to the south-west, and mount the hill
among pine woods. Glade, thicket, and grove
surround you. You follow winding sandy
tracks that lead nowhither. You see a deer;
a multitude of quail arises. But the sound
of the sea still follows you as you advance,
like that of wind among the trees, only harsher
and stranger to the ear; and when at length
you gain the summit, out breaks on every hand
and with freshened vigour, that same unending,
distant, whispering rumble of the ocean; for
now you are on the top of Monterey peninsula,

and the noise no longer only mounts to you
from behind along the beach towards Santa
Cruz, but from your right also, round by
Chinatown and Pinos lighthouse, and from
down before you to the mouth of the Car-
mello river. The whole woodland is begirt
with thundering surges. The silence that
immediately surrounds you where you stand
is not so much broken as it is haunted by
this distant, circling rumour. It sets your
senses upon edge; you strain your attention;
you are clearly and unusually conscious of
small sounds near at hand; you walk listening like an Indian hunter; and that voice
of the Pacific is a sort of disquieting company
to you in your walk.

When once I was in these woods I found it
difficult to turn homeward. All woods lure a
rambler onward; but in those of Monterey it
was the surf that particularly invited me to
prolong my walks. I would push straight for
the shore where I thought it to be nearest.
Indeed, there was scarce a direction that would
not, sooner or later, have brought me forth on
the Pacific. The emptiness of the woods gave

me a sense of freedom and discovery in these
excursions. I never in all my visits met but
one man. He was a Mexican, very dark of
hue, but smiling and fat, and he carried an axe,
though his true business at that moment was
to seek for straying cattle. I asked him what
o'clock it was, but he seemed neither to know
nor care; and when he in his turn asked me
for news of his cattle, I showed myself equally
indifferent. We stood and smiled upon each
other for a few seconds, and then turned without a word and took our several ways across
the forest.

One day—I shall never forget it—I had
taken a trail that was new to me. After a
while the woods began to open, the sea to
sound nearer hand. I came upon a road, and,
to my surprise, a stile. A step or two farther,
and, without leaving the woods, I found myself
among trim houses. I walked through street
after street, parallel and at right angles, paved
with sward and dotted with trees, but still un-
deniable streets, and each with its name posted
at the corner, as in a real town. Facing down
the main thoroughfare—'Central Avenue,' as

it was ticketed—I saw an open-air temple, with benches and sounding-board, as though for an orchestra. The houses were all tightly shuttered; there was no smoke, no sound but of the waves, no moving thing. I have never been in any place that seemed so dreamlike. Pompeii is all in a bustle with visitors, and its antiquity and strangeness deceive the imagination; but this town had plainly not been built above a year or two, and perhaps had been deserted overnight. Indeed, it was not so much like a deserted town as like a scene upon the stage by daylight, and with no one on the boards. The barking of a dog led me at last to the only house still occupied, where a Scotch pastor and his wife pass the winter alone in this empty theatre. The place was 'The Pacific Camp Grounds, the Christian Seaside Resort.' Thither, in the warm season, crowds come to enjoy a life of teetotalism, religion, and flirtation, which I am willing to think blameless and agreeable. The neighbourhood at least is well selected. The Pacific booms in front. Westward is Point Pinos, with the lighthouse in a wilderness of sand, where you will find the

lightkeeper playing the piano, making models
and bows and arrows, studying dawn and
sunrise in amateur oil-painting, and with a
dozen other elegant pursuits and interests to
surprise his brave, old-country rivals. To the
east, and still nearer, you will come upon a
space of open down, a hamlet, a haven among
rocks, a world of surge and screaming sea-
gulls. Such scenes are very similar in different
climates; they appear homely to the eyes of
all; to me this was like a dozen spots in
Scotland. And yet the boats that ride in the
haven are of strange outlandish design; and,
if you walk into the hamlet, you will behold
costumes and faces and hear a tongue that
are unfamiliar to the memory. The joss-stick
burns, the opium pipe is smoked, the floors are
strewn with slips of coloured paper—prayers,
you would say, that had somehow missed their
destination—and a man guiding his upright
pencil from right to left across the sheet, writes
home the news of Monterey to the Celestial
Empire.

The woods and the Pacific rule between
them the climate of this seaboard region. On

the streets of Monterey, when the air does not smell salt from the one, it will be blowing perfumed from the resinous tree-tops of the other. For days together a hot, dry air will overhang the town, close as from an oven, yet healthful and aromatic in the nostrils. The cause is not far to seek, for the woods are afire, and the hot wind is blowing from the hills. These fires are one of the great dangers of California. I have seen from Monterey as many as three at the same time, by day a cloud of smoke, by night a red coal of conflagration in the distance. A little thing will start them, and, if the wind be favourable, they gallop over miles of country faster than a horse. The inhabitants must turn out and work like demons, for it is not only the pleasant groves that are destroyed; the climate and the soil are equally at stake, and these fires prevent the rains of the next winter and dry up perennial fountains. California has been a land of promise in its time, like Palestine; but if the woods continue so swiftly to perish, it may become, like Palestine, a land of desolation.

To visit the woods while they are languidly

burning is a strange piece of experience. The fire passes through the underbrush at a run. Every here and there a tree flares up instantaneously from root to summit, scattering tufts of flame, and is quenched, it seems, as quickly. But this last is only in semblance. For after this first squib-like conflagration of the dry moss and twigs, there remains behind a deep-rooted and consuming fire in the very entrails of the tree. The resin of the pitch-pine is principally condensed at the base of the bole and in the spreading roots. Thus, after the light, showy, skirmishing flames, which are only as the match to the explosion, have already scampered down the wind into the distance, the true harm is but beginning for this giant of the woods. You may approach the tree from one side, and see it, scorched indeed from top to bottom, but apparently survivor of the peril. Make the circuit, and there, on the other side of the column, is a clear mass of living coal, spreading like an ulcer; while underground, to their most extended fibre, the roots are being eaten out by fire, and the smoke is rising through the fissures to the surface. A little while, and, without a

nod of warning, the huge pine-tree snaps off
short across the ground and falls prostrate with
a crash. Meanwhile the fire continues its silent
business; the roots are reduced to a fine ash;
and long afterwards, if you pass by, you will
find the earth pierced with radiating galleries,
and preserving the design of all these subter-
ranean spurs, as though it were the mould for
a new tree instead of the print of an old one.
These pitch-pines of Monterey are, with the
single exception of the Monterey cypress, the
most fantastic of forest trees. No words can
give an idea of the contortion of their growth;
they might figure without change in a circle of
the nether hell as Dante pictured it; and at
the rate at which trees grow, and at which
forest fires spring up and gallop through the
hills of California, we may look forward to a
time when there will not be one of them left
standing in that land of their nativity. At
least they have not so much to fear from the
axe, but perish by what may be called a natural
although a violent death; while it is man in
his short-sighted greed that robs the country
of the nobler red-wood. Yet a little while and

perhaps all the hills of sea-board California may be as bald as Tamalpais.

I have an interest of my own in these forest fires, for I came so near to lynching on one occasion, that a braver man might have retained a thrill from the experience. I wished to be certain whether it was the moss, that quaint funereal ornament of Californian forests, which blazed up so rapidly when the flame first touched the tree. I suppose I must have been under the influence of Satan, for instead of plucking off a piece for my experiment, what should I do but walk up to a great pine-tree in a portion of the wood which had escaped so much as scorching, strike a match, and apply the flame gingerly to one of the tassels. The tree went off simply like a rocket; in three seconds it was a roaring pillar of fire. Close by I could hear the shouts of those who were at work combating the original conflagration. I could see the waggon that had brought them tied to a live oak in a piece of open; I could even catch the flash of an axe as it swung up through the underwood into the sunlight. Had any one observed the result of my experiment my neck was literally not worth a pinch of snuff; after a few minutes of passionate expostulation I should have been run up to a convenient bough.

> To die for faction is a common evil;
> But to be hanged for nonsense is the devil.

I have run repeatedly, but never as I ran that day. At night I went out of town, and there was my own particular fire, quite distinct from the other, and burning as I thought with even greater vigour.

But it is the Pacific that exercises the most direct and obvious power upon the climate. At sunset, for months together, vast, wet, melancholy fogs arise and come shoreward from the ocean. From the hill-top above Monterey the scene is often noble, although it is always sad. The upper air is still bright with sunlight; a glow still rests upon the Gabelano Peak; but the fogs are in possession of the lower levels; they crawl in scarves among the sandhills; they float, a little higher, in clouds of a gigantic size and often of a wild configuration; to the south, where they have struck the seaward shoulder of the mountains of Santa Lucia, they double back and spire up skyward like smoke. Where their shadow touches, colour dies out of the world. The air grows chill and deadly as they advance. The trade-wind freshens, the trees begin to sigh, and all the windmills in Monterey are whirling and creaking and filling their cisterns with the brackish water of the sands. It takes but a little while till the invasion is complete. The sea, in its lighter order, has submerged the earth. Monterey is curtained in for the night in thick, wet, salt, and frigid clouds, so to remain till day returns; and before the sun's rays they slowly disperse and retreat in broken squadrons to the bosom of the sea. And yet often when the fog is thickest and most chill, a few steps out of the town and up the slope, the night will be dry and warm and full of inland perfume.

MEXICANS, AMERICANS, AND INDIANS

The history of Monterey has yet to be written. Founded by Catholic missionaries, a place of wise beneficence to Indians, a place of arms, a Mexican capital continually wrested by one faction from another, an American capital when the first House of Representatives held its deliberations, and then falling lower and lower from the capital of the State to the capital of a county, and from that again, by the loss of its charter and town lands, to a mere bankrupt village, its rise and decline is typical of that of all Mexican institutions and even Mexican families in California.

Nothing is stranger in that strange State than the rapidity with which the soil has changed hands. The Mexicans, you may say, are all poor and landless, like their former capital; and yet both it and they hold themselves apart and preserve their ancient customs and something of their ancient air.

The town, when I was there, was a place of two or three streets, economically paved with sea-sand, and two or three lanes, which were watercourses in the rainy season, and were, at all times, rent up by fissures four or five feet deep. There were no street lights. Short sections of wooden sidewalk only added to the dangers of the night, for they were often high above the level of the roadway, and no one could tell where they would be likely to begin or end.   The houses were, for the most part, built of unbaked adobe brick, many of them old for so new a country, some of very elegant proportions, with low, spacious, shapely rooms, and walls so thick that the heat of summer never dried them to the heart.   At the approach of the rainy season a deathly chill and a grave-yard smell began to hang about the lower floors; and diseases of the chest are common and fatal among house-keeping people of either sex.

There was no activity but in and around the saloons, where people sat almost all day long playing cards.   The smallest excursion was made on horseback.   You would scarcely ever see the main street without a horse or two tied to posts, and making a fine figure with their Mexican housings.   It struck me oddly to come across some of the *Cornhill* illustrations to Mr. Blackmore's *Erema*, and see all the characters astride on English saddles.   As a matter of fact, an English saddle is a rarity even in San Francisco, and, you may say, a thing unknown in all the rest of California. In a place so exclusively Mexican as Monterey, you saw not only Mexican saddles but true Vaquero riding—men always at the hand-gallop up hill and down dale, and round the sharpest corner, urging their horses with cries and gesticulations and cruel rotatory spurs, checking them dead with a touch, or wheeling them right-about-face in a square yard. The type of face and character of bearing are surprisingly un-American. The first ranged from something like the pure Spanish, to something, in its sad fixity, not unlike the pure Indian, although I do not suppose there was one pure blood of either race in all the country. As for the second, it was a matter of perpetual surprise to find, in that world of absolutely mannerless Americans, a people full of deportment, solemnly courteous, and doing all things with grace and decorum. In dress they ran to colour and bright sashes. Not even the most Americanised could always resist the temptation to stick a red rose into his hatband. Not even the most Americanised would descend to wear the vile dress hat of civilisation. Spanish was the language of the streets. It was difficult to get along without a word or two of that language for an occasion. The only communications in which the population joined were with a view to amusement. A weekly public ball took place with great etiquette, in addition to the numerous fandangoes in private houses. There was a really fair amateur brass band. Night after night serenaders would be going about the street, sometimes in a company and with several instruments and voices together, sometimes severally, each guitar before a different window. It was a strange thing to lie awake in nineteenth-century America, and hear the guitar accompany, and one of these old, heart-breaking Spanish love songs mount into the night air, perhaps in a deep baritone, perhaps in that high-pitched, pathetic, womanish alto which is so common among Mexican men, and which strikes on the unaccustomed ear as something not entirely human but altogether sad.

The town, then, was essentially and wholly Mexican; and yet almost all the land in the neighbourhood was held by Americans, and it was from the same class, numerically so small, that the principal officials were selected. This Mexican and that Mexican would describe to you his old family estates, not one rood of which remained to him. You would ask him how that came about, and elicit some tangled story back-foremost, from which you gathered that the Americans had been greedy like designing men, and the Mexicans greedy like children, but no other certain fact. Their merits and their faults contributed alike to the ruin of the former landholders. It is true they were improvident, and easily dazzled with the sight of ready money; but they were gentle-folk besides, and that in a way which curiously unfitted them to combat Yankee craft. Suppose they have a paper to sign, they would think it a reflection on the other party to examine the terms with any great minuteness; nay, suppose them to observe some doubtful clause, it is ten to one they would refuse from delicacy to object to it. I know I am speaking within the mark, for I have seen such a case occur, and the Mexican, in spite of the advice of his lawyer, has signed the imperfect paper like a lamb. To have spoken in the matter, he said, above all to have let the other party guess that he had seen a lawyer, would have 'been like doubting his word.' The scruple sounds oddly to one of ourselves, who have been brought up to understand all business as a competition in fraud, and honesty itself to be a virtue which regards the carrying out but not the creation of agreements. This single unworldly trait will account for much of that revolution of which we are speaking. The Mexicans have the name of being great swindlers, but certainly the accusation cuts both ways. In a contest of this sort, the entire booty would scarcely have passed into the hands of the more scrupulous race.

Physically the Americans have triumphed; but it is not entirely seen how far they have themselves been morally conquered. This is, of course, but a part of a part of an extraordinary problem now in the course of being solved in the various States of the American Union. I am reminded of an anecdote. Some years ago, at a great sale of wine, all the odd lots were purchased by a grocer in a small way in the old town of Edinburgh. The agent had the curiosity to visit him some time after and inquire what possible use he could have for such material. He was shown, by way of answer, a huge vat where all the liquors, from humble Gladstone to imperial Tokay, were fermenting together. 'And what,' he asked, 'do you propose to call this?' 'I'm no very sure,' replied the grocer, 'but I think it's going to turn out port.' In the older Eastern States, I think we may say that this hotch-potch of races is going to turn out English, or thereabout. But the problem is indefinitely varied in other zones. The elements are differently mingled in the south, in what we may call the Territorial belt, and in the group of States on the Pacific coast. Above all, in these last, we may look to see some monstrous hybrid— whether good or evil, who shall forecast? but certainly original and all their own. In my little restaurant at Monterey, we have sat down to table day after day, a Frenchman, two Portuguese, an Italian, a Mexican, and a Scotchman: we had for common visitors an American from Illinois, a nearly pure blood Indian woman, and a naturalised Chinese; and from time to time a Switzer and a German came down from country ranches for the night. No wonder that the Pacific coast is a foreign land to visitors from the Eastern States, for each race contributes something of its own. Even the despised Chinese have taught the youth of California, none indeed of their virtues, but the debasing use of opium. And chief among these influences is that of the Mexicans.

The Mexicans although in the State are out of it. They still preserve a sort of international independence, and keep their affairs snug to themselves. Only four or five years ago Vasquez, the bandit, his troops being dispersed and the hunt too hot for him in other parts of California, returned to his native Monterey, and was seen publicly in her streets and saloons, fearing no man. The year that I was there there occurred two reputed murders. As the Montereyans are exceptionally vile speakers of each other and of every one behind his back, it is not possible for me to judge how much truth there may have been in these reports; but in the one case every one believed, and in the other some suspected, that there had been foul play; and nobody dreamed for an instant of taking the authorities into their counsel. Now this is, of course, characteristic enough of the Mexicans; but it is a noteworthy feature that all the Americans in Monterey acquiesced without a word in this inaction. Even when I spoke to them upon the subject, they seemed not to understand my surprise; they had forgotten the traditions of their own race and upbringing, and become, in a word, wholly Mexicanised.

Again, the Mexicans, having no ready money to speak of, rely almost entirely in their business transactions upon each other's worthless paper. Pedro the penniless pays you with an I O U from the equally penniless Miguel. It is a sort of local currency by courtesy. Credit in these parts has passed into a superstition. I have seen a strong, violent man struggling for months to recover a debt, and getting nothing but an exchange of waste paper. The very storekeepers are averse to asking for cash payments, and are more surprised than pleased when they are offered. They fear there must be something under it, and that you mean to withdraw your custom from them. I have seen the enterprising chemist and stationer begging me with fervour to let my account run on, although I had my purse open in my hand; and partly from the commonness of the case, partly from some remains of that generous old Mexican tradition which made all men welcome to their tables, a person may be notoriously both unwilling and unable to pay, and still find credit for the necessaries of life in the stores of Monterey. Now this villainous habit of living upon 'tick' has grown into Californian nature. I do not mean that the American and European storekeepers of Monterey are as lax as Mexicans; I mean that American farmers in many parts of the State expect unlimited credit, and profit by it in the meanwhile, without a thought for consequences. Jew storekeepers have already learned the advantage to be gained from this; they lead on the farmer into irretrievable indebtedness, and keep him ever after as their bond-slave hopelessly grinding in the mill. So the whirligig of time brings in its revenges, and except that the Jew knows better than to foreclose, you may see Americans bound in the same chains with which they themselves had formerly bound the Mexican. It seems as if certain sorts of follies, like certain sorts of grain, were natural to the soil rather than to the race that holds and tills it for the moment.

In the meantime, however, the Americans rule in Monterey County. The new county seat, Salinas City, in the bald, corn-bearing plain under the Gabelano Peak, is a town of a purely American character. The land is held, for the most part, in those enormous tracts which are another legacy of Mexican days, and form the present chief danger and disgrace of California; and the holders are mostly of American or British birth. We have here in England no idea of the troubles and inconveniences which flow from the existence of these large landholders—land-thieves, land-sharks, or land-grabbers, they are more commonly and plainly called. Thus the townlands of Monterey are all in the hands of a single man. How they came there is

an obscure, vexatious question, and, rightly
or wrongly, the man is hated with a great
hatred.   His life has been repeatedly in
danger.   Not very long ago, I was told,
the stage was stopped and examined three
evenings in succession by disguised horsemen
thirsting for his blood.   A certain house on
the Salinas road, they say, he always passes
in his buggy at full speed, for the squatter
sent him warning long ago.   But a year
since he was publicly pointed out for death
by no less a man than Mr. Dennis Kearney.
Kearney is a man too well known in California, but a word of explanation is required
for English readers.   Originally an Irish
drayman, he rose, by his command of bad
language, to almost dictatorial authority in
the State; throned it there for six months
or so, his mouth full of oaths, gallowses, and
conflagrations; was first snuffed out last winter
by Mr. Coleman, backed by his San Francisco
Vigilantes and three gatling guns; completed
his own ruin by throwing in his lot with the
grotesque Greenbacker party; and had at last
to be rescued by his old enemies, the police,

out of the hands of his rebellious followers.
It was while he was at the top of his fortune
that Kearney visited Monterey with his battle-
cry against Chinese labour, the railroad mo-
nopolists, and the land-thieves; and his one
articulate counsel to the Montereyans was to
'hang David Jacks.' Had the town been
American, in my private opinion, this would
have been done years ago. Land is a subject
on which there is no jesting in the West, and
I have seen my friend the lawyer drive out of
Monterey to adjust a competition of titles with
the face of a captain going into battle and his
Smith-and-Wesson convenient to his hand.

On the ranche of another of these landholders you may find our old friend, the truck
system, in full operation. Men live there, year
in year out, to cut timber for a nominal wage,
which is all consumed in supplies. The longer
they remain in this desirable service the deeper
they will fall in debt—a burlesque injustice in
a new country, where labour should be precious,
and one of those typical instances which
explains the prevailing discontent and the
success of the demagogue Kearney.

In a comparison between what was and what is in California, the praisers of times past will fix upon the Indians of Carmel. The valley drained by the river so named is a true Californian valley, bare, dotted with chaparral, overlooked by quaint, unfinished hills. The Carmel runs by many pleasant farms, a clear and shallow river, loved by wading kine; and at last, as it is falling towards a quicksand and the great Pacific, passes a ruined mission on a hill. From the mission church the eye embraces a great field of ocean, and the ear is filled with a continuous sound of distant breakers on the shore. But the day of the Jesuit has gone by, the day of the Yankee has succeeded, and there is no one left to care for the converted savage. The church is roofless and ruinous, sea-breezes and sea-fogs, and the alternation of the rain and sunshine, daily widening the breaches and casting the crockets from the wall. As an antiquity in this new land, a quaint specimen of missionary architecture, and a memorial of good deeds, it had a triple claim to preservation from all thinking people; but neglect and abuse have been its

portion. There is no sign of American interference, save where a headboard has been torn
from a grave to be a mark for pistol bullets.
So it is with the Indians for whom it was
erected. Their lands, I was told, are being
yearly encroached upon by the neighbouring
American proprietor, and with that exception
no man troubles his head for the Indians of
Carmel. Only one day in the year, the day before our Guy Fawkes, the *padre* drives over the
hill from Monterey; the little sacristy, which is
the only covered portion of the church, is filled
with seats and decorated for the service; the
Indians troop together, their bright dresses
contrasting with their dark and melancholy
faces; and there, among a crowd of somewhat
unsympathetic holiday-makers, you may hear
God served with perhaps more touching
circumstances than in any other temple under
heaven. An Indian, stone-blind and about
eighty years of age, conducts the singing;
other Indians compose the choir; yet they
have the Gregorian music at their finger ends,
and pronounce the Latin so correctly that
I could follow the meaning as they sang. The

pronunciation was odd and nasal, the singing hurried and staccato. ' In sæcula sæculo-ho-horum,' they went, with a vigorous aspirate to every additional syllable. I have never seen faces more vividly lit up with joy than the faces of these Indian singers. It was to them not only the worship of God, nor an act by which they recalled and commemorated better days, but was besides an exercise of culture, where all they knew of art and letters was united and expressed. And it made a man's heart sorry for the good fathers of yore who had taught them to dig and to reap, to read and to sing, who had given them European mass-books which they still preserve and study in their cottages, and who had now passed away from all authority and influence in that land—to be succeeded by greedy land-thieves and sacrilegious pistol-shots. So ugly a thing may our Anglo-Saxon Protestantism appear beside the doings of the Society of Jesus.

But revolution in this world succeeds to revolution. All that I say in this paper is in a paulo-past tense. The Monterey of last year exists no longer. A huge hotel has sprung up in the desert by the railway. Three sets of diners sit down successively to table. Invaluable toilettes figure along the beach and between the live oaks; and Monterey is advertised in the newspapers, and posted in the waiting-rooms at railway stations, as a resort for wealth and fashion. Alas for the little town! it is not strong enough to resist the influence of the flaunting caravanserai, and the poor, quaint, penniless native gentlemen of Monterey must perish, like a lower race, before the millionaire vulgarians of the Big Bonanza.

[1880.]

III

FONTAINEBLEAU:

VILLAGE COMMUNITIES OF PAINTERS

I

THE charm of Fontainebleau is a thing apart.
It is a place that people love even more
than they admire. The vigorous forest air,
the silence, the majestic avenues of highway, the wilderness of tumbled boulders, the
great age and dignity of certain groves—
these are but ingredients, they are not the
secret of the philtre. The place is sanative;
the air, the light, the perfumes, and the
shapes of things concord in happy harmony.
The artist may be idle and not fear the
'blues.' He may dally with his life. Mirth,
lyric mirth, and a vivacious classical contentment are of the very essence of the better
kind of art; and these, in that most smiling

forest, he has the chance to learn or to remember. Even on the plain of Bière, where the Angelus of Millet still tolls upon the ear of fancy, a larger air, a higher heaven, something ancient and healthy in the face of nature, purify the mind alike from dulness and hysteria. There is no place where the young are more gladly conscious of their youth, or the old better contented with their age.

The fact of its great and special beauty further recommends this country to the artist. The field was chosen by men in whose blood there still raced some of the gleeful or solemn exultation of great art—Millet who loved dignity like Michelangelo, Rousseau whose modern brush was dipped in the glamour of the ancients. It was chosen before the day of that strange turn in the history of art, of which we now perceive the culmination in impressionistic tales and pictures—that voluntary aversion of the eye from all speciously strong and beautiful effects—that disinterested love of dulness which has set so many Peter Bells to paint the river-side primrose. It was then chosen for its proximity to Paris. And for the same cause, and by the force of tradition, the painter of to-day continues to inhabit and to paint it. There is in France scenery incomparable for romance and harmony. Provence, and the valley of the Rhone from Vienne to Tarascon, are one succession of masterpieces waiting for the brush. The beauty is not merely beauty; it tells, besides, a tale to the imagination, and surprises while it charms. Here you shall see castellated towns that would befit the scenery of dreamland; streets that glow with colour like cathedral windows; hills of the most exquisite proportions; flowers of every precious colour, growing thick like grass. All these, by the grace of railway travel, are brought to the very door of the modern painter; yet he does not seek them; he remains faithful to Fontainebleau, to the eternal bridge of Gretz, to the watering-pot cascade in Cernay valley. Even Fontainebleau was chosen for him; even in Fontainebleau he shrinks from what is sharply charactered. But one thing, at least, is certain, whatever he may choose to paint and in whatever manner, it is good for the artist to dwell among graceful shapes.

Fontainebleau, if it be but quiet scenery, is classically graceful; and though the student may look for different qualities, this quality, silently present, will educate his hand and eye.

But, before all its other advantages—charm, loveliness, or proximity to Paris—comes the great fact that it is already colonised. The institution of a painters' colony is a work of time and tact. The population must be conquered. The inn-keeper has to be taught, and he soon learns, the lesson of unlimited credit; he must be taught to welcome as a favoured guest a young gentleman in a very greasy coat, and with little baggage beyond a box of colours and a canvas; and he must learn to preserve his faith in customers who will eat heartily and drink of the best, borrow money to buy tobacco, and perhaps not pay a stiver for a year. A colour merchant has next to be attracted. A certain vogue must be given to the place, lest the painter, most gregarious of animals, should find himself alone. And no sooner are these first difficulties overcome, than fresh perils spring up upon the other side; and the bourgeois and the tourist are

knocking at the gate. This is the crucial
moment for the colony. If these intruders
gain a footing, they not only banish freedom
and amenity; pretty soon, by means of their
long purses, they will have undone the education of the innkeeper; prices will rise and
credit shorten; and the poor painter must
fare farther on and find another hamlet.
'Not here, O Apollo!' will become his song.
Thus Trouville and, the other day, St. Raphael
were lost to the arts. Curious and not always
edifying are the shifts that the French student
uses to defend his lair; like the cuttlefish,
he must sometimes blacken the waters of his
chosen pool; but at such a time and for so
practical a purpose Mrs. Grundy must allow
him licence. Where his own purse and credit
are not threatened, he will do the honours of
his village generously. Any artist is made
welcome, through whatever medium he may
seek expression; science is respected; even
the idler, if he prove, as he so rarely does, a
gentleman, will soon begin to find himself at
home. And when that essentially modern
creature, the English or American girl-student,

began to walk calmly into his favourite inns as if into a drawing-room at home, the French painter owned himself defenceless; he submitted or he fled. His French respectability, quite as precise as ours, though covering different provinces of life, recoiled aghast before the innovation. But the girls were painters; there was nothing to be done; and Barbizon, when I last saw it and for the time at least, was practically ceded to the fair invader. Paterfamilias, on the other hand, the common tourist, the holiday shopman, and the cheap young gentleman upon the spree, he hounded from his villages with every circumstance of contumely.

This purely artistic society is excellent for the young artist. The lads are mostly fools; they hold the latest orthodoxy in its crudeness; they are at that stage of education, for the most part, when a man is too much occupied with style to be aware of the necessity for any matter; and this, above all for the Englishman, is excellent. To work grossly at the trade, to forget sentiment, to think of his material and nothing else, is, for awhile at least, the king's highway of progress. Here, in England, too many painters and writers dwell dispersed, unshielded, among the intelligent bourgeois. These, when they are not merely indifferent, prate to him about the lofty aims and moral influence of art. And this is the lad's ruin. For art is, first of all and last of all, a trade. The love of words and not a desire to publish new discoveries, the love of form and not a novel reading of historical events, mark the vocation of the writer and the painter. The arabesque, properly speaking, and even in literature, is the first fancy of the artist; he first plays with his material as a child plays with a kaleidoscope; and he is already in a second stage when he begins to use his pretty counters for the end of representation. In that, he must pause long and toil faithfully; that is his apprenticeship; and it is only the few who will really grow beyond it, and go forward, fully equipped, to do the business of real art—to give life to abstractions and signifi-cance and charm to facts. In the meanwhile, let him dwell much among his fellow-craftsmen. They alone can take a serious interest in the childish tasks and pitiful successes of these years. They alone can behold with equanimity this fingering of the dumb keyboard, this polishing of empty sentences, this dull and literal painting of dull and insignificant subjects. Outsiders will spur him on. They will say, 'Why do you not write a great book? paint a great picture?' If his guardian angel fail him, they may even persuade him to the attempt, and, ten to one, his hand is coarsened and his style falsified for life.

And this brings me to a warning. The life of the apprentice to any art is both unstrained and pleasing; it is strewn with small successes in the midst of a career of failure, patiently supported; the heaviest scholar is conscious of a certain progress; and if he come not appreciably nearer to the art of Shakespeare, grows letter-perfect in the domain of A-B, ab. But the time comes when a man should cease prelusory gymnastic, stand up, put a violence upon his will, and for better or worse, begin the business of creation. This evil day there is a tendency continually to postpone: above all with painters. They have made so many studies that it has become a habit; they make more, the walls of exhibitions blush with them; and death finds these aged students still busy with their horn-book. This class of man finds a congenial home in artist villages; in the slang of the English colony at Barbizon we used to call them 'Snoozers.' Continual returns to the city, the society of men farther advanced, the study of great works, a sense of humour or, if such a thing is to be had, a little religion or philosophy, are the means of treatment. It will be time enough to think of curing the malady after it has been caught; for to catch it is the very thing for which you seek that dream-land of the painters' village. 'Snoozing' is a part of the artistic education; and the rudiments must be learned stupidly, all else being forgotten, as if they were an object in themselves.

Lastly, there is something, or there seems to be something, in the very air of France that communicates the love of style. Precision, clarity, the cleanly and crafty employment of material, a grace in the handling, apart from any value in the thought, seem to be acquired by the mere residence; or if not acquired, become at least the more appreciated. The air of Paris is alive with this technical inspiration. And to leave that airy city and awake next day upon the borders of the forest is but to change externals. The same spirit of dexterity and finish breathes from the long alleys and the lofty groves, from the wildernesses that are still pretty in their confusion, and the great plain that contrives to be decorative in its emptiness.

II

In spite of its really considerable extent, the forest of Fontainebleau is hardly anywhere tedious. I know the whole western side of it with what, I suppose, I may call thoroughness; well enough at least to testify that there is no square mile without some special character and charm. Such quarters, for instance, as the Long Rocher, the Bas-Bréau, and the Reine Blanche, might be a hundred miles apart; they have scarce a point in common beyond the silence of the birds. The two last are really conterminous; and in both are tall and ancient trees that have outlived a thousand political vicissitudes. But in the one the great oaks prosper placidly upon an even floor; they beshadow a great field; and the air and the light are very free below their stretching boughs. In the other the trees find difficult footing; castles of white rock lie tumbled one upon another, the foot slips, the crooked viper slumbers, the moss clings in the crevice; and above it all the great beech goes spiring and casting forth her arms, and, with a grace beyond church architecture, canopies this rugged chaos. Meanwhile, dividing the two cantons, the broad white causeway of the Paris road runs in an avenue: a road conceived for pageantry and for triumphal marches, an avenue for an army; but, its days of glory over, it now lies grilling in the sun between cool groves, and only at intervals the vehicle of the cruising tourist is seen far away and faintly audible along its ample sweep. A little upon one side, and you find a district of sand and birch and boulder; a little upon the other lies the valley of Apremont, all juniper and heather; and close beyond that you may

walk into a zone of pine trees. So artfully are
the ingredients mingled. Nor must it be forgotten that, in all this part, you come continually forth upon a hill-top, and behold the plain,
northward and westward, like an unrefulgent
sea; nor that all day long the shadows keep
changing; and at last, to the red fires of sunset, night succeeds, and with the night a new
forest, full of whisper, gloom, and fragrance.
There are few things more renovating than to
leave Paris, the lamplit arches of the Carrousel,
and the long alignment of the glittering streets,
and to bathe the senses in this fragrant darkness of the wood.

In this continual variety the mind is kept
vividly alive. It is a changeful place to paint,
a stirring place to live in. As fast as your foot
carries you, you pass from scene to scene, each
vigorously painted in the colours of the sun,
each endeared by that hereditary spell of forests
on the mind of man who still remembers and
salutes the ancient refuge of his race.

And yet the forest has been civilised throughout. The most savage corners bear a name,
and have been cherished like antiquities; in

the most remote, Nature has prepared and
balanced her effects as if with conscious art;
and man, with his guiding arrows of blue
paint, has countersigned the picture. After
your farthest wandering, you are never surprised to come forth upon the vast avenue of
highway, to strike the centre point of branch-
ing alleys, or to find the aqueduct trailing,
thousand-footed, through the brush. It is not
a wilderness; it is rather a preserve. And,
fitly enough, the centre of the maze is not a
hermit's cavern. In the midst, a little mirthful
town lies sunlit, humming with the business of
pleasure; and the palace, breathing distinction
and peopled by historic names, stands smoke-
less among gardens.

Perhaps the last attempt at savage life was
that of the harmless humbug who called himself the hermit. In a great tree, close by the
high-road, he had built himself a little cabin
after the manner of the Swiss Family Robinson;
thither he mounted at night, by the romantic
aid of a rope ladder; and if dirt be any proof
of sincerity, the man was savage as a Sioux.
I had the pleasure of his acquaintance; he

appeared grossly stupid, not in his perfect wits, and interested in nothing but small change; for that he had a great avidity. In the course of time he proved to be a chicken-stealer, and vanished from his perch; and perhaps from the first he was no true votary of forest freedom, but an ingenious, theatrically-minded beggar, and his cabin in the tree was only stock-in-trade to beg withal. The choice of his position would seem to indicate so much; for if in the forest there are no places still to be discovered, there are many that have been forgotten, and that lie unvisited. There, to be sure, are the blue arrows waiting to reconduct you, now blazed upon a tree, now posted in the corner of a rock. But your security from interruption is complete; you might camp for weeks, if there were only water, and not a soul suspect your presence; and if I may suppose the reader to have committed some great crime and come to me for aid, I think I could still find my way to a small cavern, fitted with a hearth and chimney, where he might lie perfectly concealed. A confederate landscape-painter might daily supply him with food;

for water, he would have to make a nightly tramp as far as to the nearest pond; and at last, when the hue and cry began to blow over, he might get gently on the train at some side station, work round by a series of junctions, and be quietly captured at the frontier.

Thus Fontainebleau, although it is truly but a pleasure-ground, and although, in favourable weather, and in the more celebrated quarters, it literally buzzes with the tourist, yet has some of the immunities and offers some of the repose of natural forests. And the solitary, although he must return at night to his frequented inn, may yet pass the day with his own thoughts in the companionable silence of the trees. The demands of the imagination vary; some can be alone in a back garden looked upon by windows; others, like the ostrich, are content with a solitude that meets the eye; and others, again, expand in fancy to the very borders of their desert, and are irritably conscious of a hunter's camp in an adjacent county. To these last, of course, Fontainebleau will seem but an extended tea-garden: a Rosherville on a by-day. But to the plain man it offers solitude: an excellent thing in itself, and a good whet for company.

III

I was for some time a consistent Barbizonian; *et ego in Arcadia vixi*, it was a pleasant season; and that noiseless hamlet lying close among the borders of the wood is for me, as for so many others, a green spot in memory. The great Millet was just dead, the green shutters of his modest house were closed; his daughters were in mourning. The date of my first visit was thus an epoch in the history of art: in a lesser way, it was an epoch in the history of the Latin Quarter. The *Petit Cénacle* was dead and buried; Murger and his crew of sponging vagabonds were all at rest from their expedients; the tradition of their real life was nearly lost; and the petrified legend of the *Vie de Bohème* had become a sort of gospel, and still gave the cue to zealous imitators. But if the book be written in rose-water, the imitation was still farther expurgated; honesty was the rule; the innkeepers gave, as I have said, almost unlimited credit; they suffered the seediest painter to depart, to take all his belongings, and to leave his bill unpaid; and if they sometimes lost, it was by English and Americans alone. At the same time, the great influx of Anglo-Saxons had begun to affect the life of the studious. There had been disputes; and, in one instance at least, the English and the Americans had made common cause to prevent a cruel pleasantry. It would be well if nations and races could communicate their qualities; but in practice when they look upon each other, they have an eye to nothing but defects. The Anglo-Saxon is essentially dishonest; the French is devoid by nature of the principle that we call 'Fair Play.' The Frenchman marvelled at the scruples of his guest, and, when that defender of innocence retired over-seas and left his bills unpaid, he marvelled once again; the good and evil were, in his eyes, part and parcel of the same eccentricity; a shrug expressed his judgment upon both.

At Barbizon there was no master, no pontiff
in the arts.   Palizzi bore rule at Gretz—urbane,
superior rule—his memory rich in anecdotes of
the great men of yore, his mind fertile in
theories; sceptical, composed, and venerable to
the eye; and yet beneath these outworks, all
twittering with Italian superstition, his eye
scouting for omens, and the whole fabric of his
manners giving way on the appearance of a
hunchback.   Cernay had Pelouse, the admirable, placid Pelouse, smilingly critical of youth,
who, when a full-blown commercial traveller
suddenly threw down his samples, bought a
colour-box, and became the master whom we
have all admired.   Marlotte, for a central
figure, boasted Olivier de Penne.   Only Barbizon, since the death of Millet, was a headless
commonwealth.   Even its secondary lights, and
those who in my day made the stranger
welcome, have since deserted it.   The good
Lachèvre has departed, carrying his household
gods; and long before that Gaston Lafenestre
was taken from our midst by an untimely
death.   He died before he had deserved
success; it may be, he would never have

deserved it; but his kind, comely, modest countenance still haunts the memory of all who knew him. Another—whom I will not name —has moved farther on, pursuing the strange Odyssey of his decadence. His days of royal favour had departed even then; but he still retained, in his narrower life at Barbizon, a certain stamp of conscious importance, hearty, friendly, filling the room, the occupant of several chairs; nor had he yet ceased his losing battle, still labouring upon great canvases that none would buy, still waiting the return of fortune. But these days also were too good to last; and the former favourite of two sovereigns fled, if I heard the truth, by night. There was a time when he was counted a great man, and Millet but a dauber; behold, how the whirligig of time brings in his revenges! To pity Millet is a piece of arrogance; if life be hard for such resolute and pious spirits, it is harder still for us, had we the wit to understand it; but we may pity his unhappier rival, who, for no apparent merit, was raised to opulence and momentary fame, and, through no apparent fault, was suffered step by step to sink again to nothing.

No misfortune can exceed the bitterness of
such back-foremost progress, even bravely supported as it was; but to those also who were
taken early from the easel, a regret is due.
From all the young men of this period, one
stood out by the vigour of his promise; he was
in the age of fermentation, enamoured of
eccentricities. 'Il faut faire de la peinture
nouvelle,' was his watchword; but if time and
experience had continued his education, if he
had been granted health to return from these
excursions to the steady and the central, I must
believe that the name of Hills had become
famous.

Siron's inn, that excellent artists' barrack,
was managed upon easy principles. At any
hour of the night, when you returned from
wandering in the forest, you went to the bil-
liard-room and helped yourself to liquors, or
descended to the cellar and returned laden with
beer or wine. The Sirons were all locked in
slumber; there was none to check your in-
roads; only at the week's end a computation
was made, the gross sum was divided, and a
varying share set down to every lodger's name

under the rubric: *estrats*. Upon the more
long-suffering the larger tax was levied; and
your bill lengthened in a direct proportion to
the easiness of your disposition. At any hour
of the morning, again, you could get your coffee
or cold milk, and set forth into the forest. The
doves had perhaps wakened you, fluttering into
your chamber; and on the threshold of the inn
you were met by the aroma of the forest.
Close by were the great aisles, the mossy
boulders, the interminable field of forest shadow.
There you were free to dream and wander.
And at noon, and again at six o'clock, a good
meal awaited you on Siron's table. The whole
of your accommodation, set aside that varying
item of the *estrats*, cost you five francs a day;
your bill was never offered you until you asked
it; and if you were out of luck's way, you
might depart for where you pleased and leave
it pending.

IV

Theoretically, the house was open to all
comers; practically, it was a kind of club.

The guests protected themselves, and, in so
doing, they protected Siron. Formal manners
being laid aside, essential courtesy was the
more rigidly exacted; the new arrival had to
feel the pulse of the society; and a breach
of its undefined observances was promptly
punished. A man might be as plain, as dull,
as slovenly, as free of speech as he desired;
but to a touch of presumption or a word of
hectoring these free Barbizonians were as
sensitive as a tea-party of maiden ladies. I
have seen people driven forth from Barbizon;
it would be difficult to say in words what they
had done, but they deserved their fate. They
had shown themselves unworthy to enjoy these
corporate freedoms; they had pushed themselves; they had 'made their head'; they
wanted tact to appreciate the 'fine shades' of
Barbizonian etiquette. And once they were
condemned, the process of extrusion was ruth-
less in its cruelty; after one evening with the
formidable Bodmer, the Baily of our commonwealth, the erring stranger was beheld no more;
he rose exceeding early the next day, and
the first coach conveyed him from the scene

of his discomfiture. These sentences of banish-
ment were never, in my knowledge, delivered
against an artist; such would, I believe, have
been illegal; but the odd and pleasant fact
is this, that they were never needed. Painters,
sculptors, writers, singers, I have seen all of
these in Barbizon; and some were sulky, and
some blatant and inane; but one and all entered
at once into the spirit of the association. This
singular society is purely French, a creature
of French virtues, and possibly of French
defects. It cannot be imitated by the English.
The roughness, the impatience, the more
obvious selfishness, and even the more ardent
friendships of the Anglo-Saxon, speedily dis-
member such a commonwealth. But this
random gathering of young French painters,
with neither apparatus nor parade of govern-
ment, yet kept the life of the place upon a
certain footing, insensibly imposed their etiquette upon the docile, and by caustic speech
enforced their edicts against the unwelcome.
To think of it is to wonder the more at the
strange failure of their race upon the larger
theatre. This inbred civility—to use the word

in its completest meaning—this natural and
facile adjustment of contending liberties, seems
all that is required to make a governable nation
and a just and prosperous country.

Our society, thus purged and guarded, was
full of high spirits, of laughter, and of the
initiative of youth. The few elder men who
joined us were still young at heart, and took
the key from their companions. We returned
from long stations in the fortifying air, our
blood renewed by the sunshine, our spirits
refreshed by the silence of the forest; the
Babel of loud voices sounded good; we fell to
eat and play like the natural man; and in the
high inn chamber, panelled with indifferent
pictures and lit by candles guttering in the
night air, the talk and laughter sounded far
into the night. It was a good place and a
good life for any naturally-minded youth;
better yet for the student of painting, and
perhaps best of all for the student of letters.
He, too, was saturated in this atmosphere of
style; he was shut out from the disturbing
currents of the world, he might forget that
there existed other and more pressing interests

than that of art. But, in such a place, it was
hardly possible to write; he could not drug
his conscience, like the painter, by the pro-
duction of listless studies; he saw himself idle
among many who were apparently, and some
who were really, employed; and what with
the impulse of increasing health and the continual provocation of romantic scenes, he
became tormented with the desire to work.
He enjoyed a strenuous idleness full of visions,
hearty meals, long, sweltering walks, mirth
among companions; and still floating like
music through his brain, foresights of great
works that Shakespeare might be proud to
have conceived, headless epics, glorious torsos
of dramas, and words that were alive with
import. So in youth, like Moses from the
mountain, we have sights of that House
Beautiful of art which we shall never enter.
They are dreams and unsubstantial; visions
of style that repose upon no base of human
meaning; the last heart-throbs of that excited
amateur who has to die in all of us before the
artist can be born. But they come to us in
such a rainbow of glory that all subsequent

achievement appears dull and earthly in comparison. We were all artists; almost all in the age of illusion, cultivating an imaginary genius, and walking to the strains of some deceiving Ariel; small wonder, indeed, if we were happy! But art, of whatever nature, is a kind mistress; and though these dreams of youth fall by their own baselessness, others succeed, graver and more substantial; the symptoms change, the amiable malady endures; and still, at an equal distance, the House Beautiful shines upon its hill-top.

V

Gretz lies out of the forest, down by the bright river. It boasts a mill, an ancient church, a castle, and a bridge of many sterlings. And the bridge is a piece of public property; anonymously famous; beaming on the incurious dilettante from the walls of a hundred exhibitions. I have seen it in the Salon; I have seen it in the Academy; I have seen it in the last French Exposition, excellently done by Bloomer; in a black-and-white, by Mr. A. Henley, it once adorned this essay in the pages of the *Magazine of Art*. Long-suffering bridge! And if you visit Gretz to-morrow, you shall find another generation, camped at the bottom of Chevillon's garden under their white umbrellas, and doggedly painting it again.

The bridge taken for granted, Gretz is a less inspiring place than Barbizon. I give it the palm over Cernay. There is something ghastly in the great empty village square of Cernay, with the inn tables standing in one corner, as though the stage were set for rustic opera, and in the early morning all the painters breaking their fast upon white wine under the windows of the villagers. It is vastly different to awake in Gretz, to go down the green inn-garden, to find the river streaming through the bridge, and to see the dawn begin across the poplared level. The meals are laid in the cool arbour, under fluttering leaves. The splash of oars and bathers, the bathing costumes out to dry, the trim canoes beside the jetty, tell of a society that has an eye to pleasure. There is 'something to do' at Gretz. Perhaps, for that very reason, I can recall no such enduring ardours, no such glories of exhilaration, as among the solemn groves and uneventful hours of Barbizon. This 'something to do' is a great enemy to joy; it is a way out of it; you wreak your high spirits on some cut-and-dry employment, and behold them gone! But Gretz is a merry place after its kind: pretty to see, merry to inhabit. The course of its pellucid river, whether up or down, is full of gentle attractions for the navigator: islanded reed-mazes where, in autumn, the red berries cluster; the mirrored and inverted images of trees; lilies, and mills, and the foam and thunder of weirs. And of all noble sweeps of roadway, none is nobler, on a windy dusk, than the high road to Nemours between its lines of talking poplar.

But even Gretz is changed. The old inn, long shored and trussed and buttressed, fell at length under the mere weight of years, and the place as it was is but a fading image in the memory of former guests. They, indeed, recall the ancient wooden stair; they recall the rainy evening, the wide hearth, the blaze of the twig fire, and the company that gathered round the pillar in the kitchen. But the material fabric is now dust; soon, with the last of its inhabitants, its very memory shall follow; and they, in their turn, shall suffer the same law, and, both in name and lineament, vanish from the world of men. 'For remembrance of the old house' sake,' as Pepys once quaintly put it, let me tell one story. When the tide of invasion swept over France, two foreign painters were left stranded and penniless in Gretz; and there, until the war was over, the Chevillons ungrudgingly harboured them. It was difficult to obtain supplies; but the two waifs were still welcome to the best, sat down daily with the family to table, and at the due intervals were supplied with clean napkins, which they scrupled to employ. Madame Chevillon observed the fact and reprimanded them. But they stood firm; eat they must, but having no money they would soil no napkins.

VI

Nemours and Moret, for all they are so picturesque, have been little visited by painters. They are, indeed, too populous; they have manners of their own, and might resist the drastic process of colonisation. Montigny has been somewhat strangely neglected, I never knew it inhabited but once, when Will H. Low installed himself there with a barrel of *piquette*, and entertained his friends in a leafy trellis above the weir, in sight of the green country and to the music of the falling water. It was a most airy, quaint, and pleasant place of residence, just too rustic to be stagey; and from my memories of the place in general, and that garden trellis in particular—at morning, visited by birds, or at night, when the dew fell and the stars were of the party—I am inclined to think perhaps too favourably of the future of Montigny. Chailly-en-Bière has outlived all things, and lies dustily slumbering in the plain—the cemetery of itself. The great road remains to testify of its former bustle of postilions and carriage bells; and, like memorial tablets, there still hang in the inn room the paintings of a former generation, dead or decorated long ago. In my time, one man only, greatly daring, dwelt there. From time to time he would walk over to Barbizon, like a shade revisiting the glimpses of the moon, and after some communication with flesh and blood return to his austere hermitage. But even he, when I last revisited the forest, had come to Barbizon for good, and closed the roll of Chaillyites. It may revive— but I much doubt it. Achères and Recloses still wait a pioneer; Bourron is out of the question, being merely Gretz over again, without the river, the bridge, or the beauty; and of all the possible places on the western side, Marlotte alone remains to be discussed. I scarcely know Marlotte, and, very likely for that reason, am not much in love with it. It seems a glaring and unsightly hamlet. The inn of Mother Antonie is unattractive; and its more reputable rival, though comfortable enough, is commonplace. Marlotte has a name; it is famous; if I were the young painter I would leave it alone in its glory.

VII

These are the words of an old stager; and though time is a good conservative in forest places, much may be untrue to-day. Many of us have passed Arcadian days there and moved

on, but yet left a portion of our souls behind
us buried in the woods. I would not dig
for these reliquiæ; they are incommunicable
treasures that will not enrich the finder; and
yet there may lie, interred below great oaks or
scattered along forest paths, stores of youth's
dynamite and dear remembrances. And as
one generation passes on and renovates the
field of tillage for the next, I entertain a fancy
that when the young men of to-day go forth
into the forest they shall find the air still
vitalised by the spirits of their predecessors,
and, like those 'unheard melodies' that are the
sweetest of all, the memory of our laughter
shall still haunt the field of trees. Those
merry voices that in woods call the wanderer
farther, those thrilling silences and whispers of
the groves, surely in Fontainebleau they must
be vocal of me and my companions? We are
not content to pass away entirely from the
scenes of our delight; we would leave, if but
in gratitude, a pillar and a legend.

One generation after another fall like honey-
bees upon this memorable forest, rifle its sweets,
pack themselves with vital memories, and when

the theft is consummated depart again into
life richer, but poorer also. The forest, indeed,
they have possessed, from that day forward it
is theirs indissolubly, and they will return to
walk in it at night in the fondest of their
dreams, and use it for ever in their books and
pictures. Yet when they made their packets,
and put up their notes and sketches, something,
it should seem, had been forgotten. A projection of themselves shall appear to haunt
unfriended these scenes of happiness, a natural
child of fancy, begotten and forgotten unawares.
Over the whole field of our wanderings such
fetches are still travelling like indefatigable
bagmen; but the imps of Fontainebleau, as of
all beloved spots, are very long of life, and
memory is piously unwilling to forget their
orphanage. If anywhere about that wood you
meet my airy bantling, greet him with tender-
ness. He was a pleasant lad, though now
abandoned. And when it comes to your own
turn to quit the forest may you leave behind
you such another; no Antony or Werther,
let us hope, no tearful whipster, but, as be-
comes this not uncheerful and most active

age in which we figure, the child of happy hours.

No art, it may be said, was ever perfect, and not many noble, that has not been mirthfully conceived. And no man, it may be added, was ever anything but a wet blanket and a cross to his companions who boasted not a copious spirit of enjoyment. Whether as man or artist, let the youth make haste to Fontainebleau, and once there let him address himself to the spirit of the place; he will learn more from exercise than from studies, although both are necessary; and if he can get into his heart the gaiety and inspiration of the woods he will have gone far to undo the evil of his sketches. A spirit once well strung up to the concert-pitch of the primeval out-of-doors will hardly dare to finish a study and magniloquently ticket it a picture. The incommunicable thrill of things, that is the tuning-fork by which we test the flatness of our art. Here it is that Nature teaches and condemns, and still spurs up to further effort and new failure. Thus it is that she sets us blushing at our ignorant and tepid works; and the more we find of these inspiring shocks the less shall we be apt to love the literal in our productions. In all sciences and senses the letter kills; and to-day, when cackling human geese express their ignorant condemnation of all studio pictures, it is a lesson most useful to be learnt. Let the young painter go to Fontainebleau, and while he stupefies himself with studies that teach him the mechanical side of his trade, let him walk in the great air, and be a servant of mirth, and not pick and botanise, but wait upon the moods of nature. So he will learn—or learn not to forget—the poetry of life and earth, which, when he has acquired his track, will save him from joyless reproduction.

[1882.]

IV

EPILOGUE

TO 'AN INLAND VOYAGE'[1]

THE country where they journeyed, that green, breezy valley of the Loing, is one very attractive to cheerful and solitary people. The weather was superb; all night it thundered and lightened, and the rain fell in sheets; by day, the heavens were cloudless, the sun fervent, the air vigorous and pure. They walked separate: the Cigarette plodding behind with some philosophy, the lean Arethusa posting on ahead. Thus each enjoyed his own reflections by the way; each had perhaps time to tire of them before he met his comrade at the designated inn; and the pleasures of society and solitude combined to fill the day. The Are-

[1] See *An Inland Voyage*, by Robert Louis Stevenson, 1878.

thusa carried in his knapsack the works of
Charles of Orleans, and employed some of the
hours of travel in the concoction of English
roundels. In this path, he must thus have
preceded Mr. Lang, Mr. Dobson, Mr. Henley,
and all contemporary roundeleers; but for good
reasons, he will be the last to publish the result.
The Cigarette walked burthened with a volume
of Michelet. And both these books, it will
be seen, played a part in the subsequent adventure.

The Arethusa was unwisely dressed. He is
no precisian in attire; but by all accounts, he
was never so ill-inspired as on that tramp;
having set forth indeed, upon a moment's
notice, from the most unfashionable spot in
Europe, Barbizon. On his head, he wore a
smoking-cap of Indian work, the gold lace
pitifully frayed and tarnished. A flannel shirt
of an agreeable dark hue, which the satirical
called black; a light tweed coat made by a
good English tailor; ready-made cheap linen
trousers and leathern gaiters completed his
array. In person, he is exceptionally lean;
and his face is not like those of happier

mortals, a certificate. For years he could not pass a frontier or visit a bank without suspicion; the police everywhere, but in his native city, looked askance upon him; and (though I am sure it will not be credited) he is actually denied admittance to the casino of Monte Carlo. If you will imagine him, dressed as above, stooping under his knapsack, walking nearly five miles an hour with the folds of the ready-made trousers fluttering about his spindle shanks, and still looking eagerly round him as if in terror of pursuit—the figure, when realised, is far from reassuring. When Villon journeyed (perhaps by the same pleasant valley) to his exile at Roussillon, I wonder if he had not something of the same appearance. Something of the same preoccupation he had beyond a doubt, for he too must have tinkered verses as he walked, with more success than his successor. And if he had anything like the same inspiring weather, the same nights of uproar, men in armour rolling and resounding down the stairs of heaven, the rain hissing on the village streets, the wild bull's-eye of the storm flashing all night long into the bare inn-chamber—the same sweet return of day, the same unfathomable blue of noon, the same high-coloured, halcyon eves—and above all if he had anything like as good a comrade, anything like as keen a relish for what he saw, and what he ate, and the rivers that he bathed in, and the rubbish that he wrote, I would exchange estates to-day with the poor exile, and count myself a gainer.

But there was another point of similarity between the two journeys, for which the Arethusa was to pay dear: both were gone upon in days of incomplete security. It was not long after the Franco-Prussian war. Swiftly as men forget, that country-side was still alive with tales of uhlans, and outlying sentries, and hairbreadth 'scapes from the ignominious cord, and pleasant momentary friendships between invader and invaded. A year, at the most two years later, you might have tramped all that country over and not heard one anecdote. And a year or two later, you would—if you were a rather ill-looking young man in nondescript array—have gone your rounds in greater safety; for along with more interesting matter, the Prussian spy would have somewhat faded from men's imaginations.

For all that, our voyager had got beyond Château Renard before he was conscious of arousing wonder. On the road between that place and Châtillon-sur-Loing, however, he encountered a rural postman; they fell together in talk, and spoke of a variety of subjects; but through one and all, the postman was still visibly preoccupied, and his eyes were faithful to the Arethusa's knapsack. At last, with mysterious roguishness, he inquired what it contained, and on being answered, shook his head with kindly incredulity. '*Non*,' said he, '*non, vous avez des portraits.*' And then with a languishing appeal, '*Voyons*, show me the portraits!' It was some little while before the Arethusa, with a shout of laughter, recognised his drift. By portraits he meant indecent photographs; and in the Arethusa, an austere and rising author, he thought to have identified a pornographic colporteur. When country-folk in France have made up their minds as to a person's calling, argument is fruitless. Along all the rest of the way, the postman piped and

fluted meltingly to get a sight of the collection; now he would upbraid, now he would
reason—' *Voyons*, I will tell nobody'; then he
tried corruption, and insisted on paying for a
glass of wine; and, at last, when their ways
separated—'*Non*,' said he, '*ce n'est pas bien de
votre part. O non, ce n'est pas bien.*' And
shaking his head with quite a sentimental sense
of injury, he departed unrefreshed.

On certain little difficulties encountered by
the Arethusa at Châtillon-sur-Loing, I have
not space to dwell; another Châtillon, of
grislier memory, looms too near at hand. But
the next day, in a certain hamlet called La
Jussière, he stopped to drink a glass of syrup
in a very poor, bare drinking shop. The
hostess, a comely woman, suckling a child,
examined the traveller with kindly and pitying
eyes. 'You are not of this department?' she
asked. The Arethusa told her he was English.
'Ah!' she said, surprised. 'We have no
English. We have many Italians, however,
and they do very well; they do not complain
of the people of hereabouts. An Englishman
may do very well also; it will be something

new.' Here was a dark saying, over which the Arethusa pondered as he drank his grenadine; but when he rose and asked what was to pay, the light came upon him in a flash. '*O, pour vous,*' replied the landlady, 'a halfpenny!' *Pour vous?* By heaven, she took him for a beggar! He paid his halfpenny, feeling that it were ungracious to correct her. But when he was forth again upon the road, he became vexed in spirit. The conscience is no gentleman, he is a rabbinical fellow; and his conscience told him he had stolen the syrup.

That night the travellers slept in Gien; the next day they passed the river and set forth (severally, as their custom was) on a short stage through the green plain upon the Berry side, to Châtillon-sur-Loire. It was the first day of the shooting; and the air rang with the report of firearms and the admiring cries of sportsmen. Overhead the birds were in consternation, wheeling in clouds, settling and re-arising. And yet with all this bustle on either hand, the road itself lay solitary. The Arethusa smoked a pipe beside a milestone, and I remember he laid down very exactly all he was to do at

Châtillon: how he was to enjoy a cold plunge, to change his shirt, and to await the Cigarette's arrival, in sublime inaction, by the margin of the Loire. Fired by these ideas, he pushed the more rapidly forward, and came, early in the afternoon and in a breathing heat, to the entering-in of that ill-fated town. Childe Roland to the dark tower came.

A polite gendarme threw his shadow on the path.

' *Monsieur est voyageur?* ' he asked.

And the Arethusa, strong in his innocence, forgetful of his vile attire, replied—I had almost said with gaiety: 'So it would appear.'

'His papers are in order?' said the gendarme. And when the Arethusa, with a slight change of voice, admitted he had none, he was informed (politely enough) that he must appear before the Commissary.

The Commissary sat at a table in his bedroom, stripped to the shirt and trousers, but still copiously perspiring; and when he turned upon the prisoner a large meaningless countenance, that was (like Bardolph's) 'all whelks and bubuckles,' the dullest might have been prepared for grief. Here was a stupid man, sleepy with the heat and fretful at the interruption, whom neither appeal nor argument could reach.

THE COMMISSARY. You have no papers?

THE ARETHUSA. Not here.

THE COMMISSARY. Why?

THE ARETHUSA. I have left them behind in my valise.

THE COMMISSARY. You know, however, that it is forbidden to circulate without papers?

THE ARETHUSA. Pardon me: I am convinced of the contrary. I am here on my rights as an English subject by international treaty.

THE COMMISSARY (*with scorn*). You call yourself an Englishman?

THE ARETHUSA. I do.

THE COMMISSARY. Humph.— What is your trade?

THE ARETHUSA. I am a Scotch Advocate.

THE COMMISSARY (*with singular annoyance*). A Scotch advocate! Do you then pretend to support yourself by that in this department?

The Arethusa modestly disclaimed the pretension. The Commissary had scored a point.

THE COMMISSARY. Why, then, do you travel?

THE ARETHUSA. I travel for pleasure.

THE COMMISSARY (*pointing to the knapsack, and with sublime incredulity*). *Avec ça? Voyez-vous, je suis un homme intelligent!* (With that? Look here, I am a person of intelligence!)

The culprit remaining silent under this home thrust, the Commissary relished his triumph for a while, and then demanded (like the postman, but with what different expectations!) to see the contents of the knapsack. And here the Arethusa, not yet sufficiently awake to his position, fell into a grave mistake. There was little or no furniture in the room except the Commissary's chair and table; and to facilitate matters, the Arethusa (with all the innocence on earth) leant the knapsack on a corner of the bed. The Commissary fairly bounded from his seat; his face and neck flushed past purple, almost into blue; and he screamed to lay the desecrating object on the floor.

The knapsack proved to contain a change of shirts, of shoes, of socks, and of linen trousers, a small dressing-case, a piece of soap in one of the shoes, two volumes of the *Collection Jannet* lettered *Poésies de Charles d'Orléans*, a map, and a version book containing divers notes in prose and the remarkable English roundels of the voyager, still to this day unpublished: the Commissary of Châtillon is the only living man who has clapped an eye on these artistic trifles. He turned the assortment over with a contumelious finger; it was plain from his daintiness that he regarded the Arethusa and all his belongings as the very temple of infection. Still there was nothing suspicious about the map, nothing really criminal except the roundels; as for Charles of Orleans, to the ignorant mind of the prisoner, he seemed as good as a certificate; and it was supposed the farce was nearly over.

The inquisitor resumed his seat.

THE COMMISSARY (*after a pause*). *Eh bien, je vais vous dire ce que vous êtes. Vous êtes allemand et vous venez chanter à la foire.* (Well, then, I will tell you what you are. You are a German and have come to sing at the fair.)

THE ARETHUSA. Would you like to hear

me sing? I believe I could convince you of the contrary.

THE COMMISSARY. *Pas de plaisanterie, monsieur!*

THE ARETHUSA. Well, sir, oblige me at least by looking at this book. Here, I open it with my eyes shut. Read one of these songs —read this one—and tell me, you who are a man of intelligence, if it would be possible to sing it at a fair?

THE COMMISSARY (*critically*). *Mais oui. Très bien.*

THE ARETHUSA. *Comment, monsieur!* What! But you do not observe it is antique. It is difficult to understand, even for you and me; but for the audience at a fair, it would be meaningless.

THE COMMISSARY (*taking a pen*). *Enfin, il faut en finir.* What is your name?

THE ARETHUSA (*speaking with the swallowing vivacity of the English*). Robert-Louis-Stev'ns'n.

THE COMMISSARY (*aghast*). *Hé! Quoi?*

THE ARETHUSA (*perceiving and improving his advantage*). Rob'rt-Lou's-Stev'ns'n.

THE COMMISSARY (*after several conflicts with his pen*). *Eh bien, il faut se passer du nom. Ça ne s'écrit pas.* (Well, we must do without the name : it is unspellable.)

The above is a rough summary of this momentous conversation, in which I have been chiefly careful to preserve the plums of the Commissary ; but the remainder of the scene, perhaps because of his rising anger, has left but little definite in the memory of the Arethusa. The Commissary was not, I think, a practised literary man; no sooner, at least, had he taken pen in hand and embarked on the composition of the *procès-verbal*, than he became distinctly more uncivil and began to show a predilection for that simplest of all forms of repartee : 'You lie!' Several times the Arethusa let it pass, and then suddenly flared up, refused to accept more insults or to answer further questions, defied the Commissary to do his worst, and promised him, if he did, that he should bitterly repent it. Perhaps if he had worn this proud front from the first, instead of beginning with a sense of entertainment and then going on to argue, the thing might have turned otherwise ;

for even at this eleventh hour the Commissary
was visibly staggered. But it was too late; he
had been challenged; the *procès-verbal* was
begun; and he again squared his elbows over
his writing, and the Arethusa was led forth a
prisoner.

A step or two down the hot road stood the
gendarmerie. Thither was our unfortunate
conducted, and there he was bidden to empty
forth the contents of his pockets. A handkerchief, a pen, a pencil, a pipe and tobacco,
matches, and some ten francs of change: that
was all. Not a file, not a cipher, not a scrap
of writing whether to identify or to condemn.
The very gendarme was appalled before such
destitution.

'I regret,' he said, 'that I arrested you, for
I see that you are no *voyou*.' And he promised
him every indulgence.

The Arethusa, thus encouraged, asked for
his pipe. That he was told was impossible,
but if he chewed, he might have some tobacco.
He did not chew, however, and asked instead
to have his handkerchief.

'*Non*,' said the gendarme. '*Nous avons eu*

des histoires de gens qui se sont pendus.' (No, we have had histories of people who hanged themselves.)

'What,' cried the Arethusa. 'And is it for that you refuse me my handkerchief? But see how much more easily I could hang myself in my trousers!'

The man was struck by the novelty of the idea; but he stuck to his colours, and only continued to repeat vague offers of service.

'At least,' said the Arethusa, 'be sure that you arrest my comrade; he will follow me ere long on the same road, and you can tell him by the sack upon his shoulders.'

This promised, the prisoner was led round into the back court of the building, a cellar door was opened, he was motioned down the stair, and bolts grated and chains clanged behind his descending person.

The philosophic and still more the imaginative mind is apt to suppose itself prepared for any mortal accident. Prison, among other ills, was one that had been often faced by the undaunted Arethusa. Even as he went down the stairs, he was telling himself that here was a famous occasion for a roundel, and that like the committed linnets of the tuneful cavalier, he too would make his prison musical. I will tell the truth at once: the roundel was never written, or it should be printed in this place, to raise a smile. Two reasons interfered: the first moral, the second physical.

It is one of the curiosities of human nature, that although all men are liars, they can none of them bear to be told so of themselves. To get and take the lie with equanimity is a stretch beyond the stoic; and the Arethusa, who had been surfeited upon that insult, was blazing inwardly with a white heat of smothered wrath. But the physical had also its part. The cellar in which he was confined was some feet underground, and it was only lighted by an unglazed, narrow aperture high up in the wall and smothered in the leaves of a green vine. The walls were of naked masonry, the floor of bare earth; by way of furniture there was an earthenware basin, a water-jug, and a wooden bedstead with a blue-gray cloak for bedding. To be taken from the hot air of a summer's afternoon, the reverberation of the road and the stir of rapid exercise, and plunged into the gloom and damp of this receptacle for vagabonds, struck an instant chill upon the Arethusa's blood. Now see in how small a matter a hardship may consist: the floor was exceedingly uneven underfoot, with the very spade-marks, I suppose, of the labourers who dug the foundations of the barrack; and what with the poor twilight and the irregular surface, walking was impossible. The caged author resisted for a good while; but the chill of the place struck deeper and deeper; and at length, with such reluctance as you may fancy, he was driven to climb upon the bed and wrap himself in the public covering. There, then, he lay upon the verge of shivering, plunged in semi-darkness, wound in a garment whose touch he dreaded like the plague, and (in a spirit far removed from resignation) telling the roll of the insults he had just received. These are not circumstances favourable to the muse.

Meantime (to look at the upper surface where the sun was still shining and the guns of sportsmen were still noisy through the tufted plain) the Cigarette was drawing near at his

more philosophic pace.   In those days of liberty
and health he was the constant partner of the
Arethusa, and had ample opportunity to share
in that gentleman's disfavour with the police.
Many a bitter bowl had he partaken of with
that disastrous comrade.   He was himself a
man born to float easily through life, his face
and manner artfully recommending him to all.
There was but one suspicious circumstance he
could not carry off, and that was his companion.
He will not readily forget the Commissary in
what is ironically called the free town of
Frankfort-on-the-Main; nor the Franco-Belgian
frontier; nor the inn at La Fère; last, but not
least, he is pretty certain to remember Châtillon-
sur-Loire.

At the town entry, the gendarme culled him
like a wayside flower; and a moment later, two
persons, in a high state of surprise, were con-
fronted in the Commissary's office.   For if the
Cigarette was surprised to be arrested, the
Commissary was no less taken aback by the
appearance and appointments of his captive.
Here was a man about whom there could be no
mistake: a man of an unquestionable and un-

assailable manner, in apple-pie order, dressed not with neatness merely but elegance, ready with his passport, at a word, and well supplied with money : a man the Commissary would have doffed his hat to on chance upon the highway ; and this *beau cavalier* unblushingly claimed the Arethusa for his comrade ! The conclusion of the interview was foregone ; of its humours, I remember only one. 'Baronet?' demanded the magistrate, glancing up from the passport. '*Alors, monsieur, vous êtes le fils d'un baron ?*' And when the Cigarette (his one mistake throughout the interview) denied the soft impeachment, '*Alors,*' from the Commissary, '*ce n'est pas votre passeport !*' But these were ineffectual thunders ; he never dreamed of laying hands upon the Cigarette ; presently he fell into a mood of unrestrained admiration, gloating over the contents of the knapsack, commending our friend's tailor. Ah, what an honoured guest was the Commissary entertaining ! what suitable clothes he wore for the warm weather ! what beautiful maps, what an attractive work of history he carried in his knapsack ! You are to understand there was now but one point of difference between them : what was to be done with the Arethusa ? the Cigarette demanding his release, the Commissary still claiming him as the dungeon's own. Now it chanced that the Cigarette had passed some years of his life in Egypt, where he had made acquaintance with two very bad things, cholera morbus and pashas; and in the eye of the Commissary, as he fingered the volume of Michelet, it seemed to our traveller there was something Turkish. I pass over this lightly; it is highly possible there was some misunderstanding, highly possible that the Commissary (charmed with his visitor) supposed the attraction to be mutual and took for an act of growing friendship what the Cigarette himself regarded as a bribe. And at any rate, was there ever a bribe more singular than an odd volume of Michelet's history ? The work was promised him for the morrow, before our departure; and presently after, either because he had his price, or to show that he was not the man to be behind in friendly offices—'*Eh bien,*' he said, '*je suppose qu'il faut lâcher votre camarade.*' And he tore up that feast of humour, the unfinished *procès-*

verbal. Ah, if he had only torn up instead the
Arethusa's roundels ! There were many works
burnt at Alexandria, there are many treasured
in the British Museum, that I could better spare
than the *procès-verbal* of Châtillon. Poor bu-
buckled Commissary ! I begin to be sorry that
he never had his Michelet : perceiving in him
fine human traits, a broad-based stupidity, a
gusto in his magisterial functions, a taste for
letters, a ready admiration for the admirable.
And if he did not admire the Arethusa, he was
not alone in that.

To the imprisoned one, shivering under the
public covering, there came suddenly a noise of
bolts and chains. He sprang to his feet, ready
to welcome a companion in calamity ; and
instead of that, the door was flung wide, the
friendly gendarme appeared above in the strong
daylight, and with a magnificent gesture (being
probably a student of the drama)—' *Vous êtes
libre !* ' he said. None too soon for the Arethusa. I doubt if he had been half an hour
imprisoned ; but by the watch in a man's brain
(which was the only watch he carried) he should
have been eight times longer ; and he passed

forth with ecstasy up the cellar stairs into the
healing warmth of the afternoon sun; and the
breath of the earth came as sweet as a cow's
into his nostril; and he heard again (and could
have laughed for pleasure) the concord of
delicate noises that we call the hum of life.

And here it might be thought that my history ended; but not so, this was an act-drop
and not the curtain. Upon what followed in
front of the barrack, since there was a lady in
the case, I scruple to expatiate. The wife of
the Maréchal-des-logis was a handsome woman,
and yet the Arethusa was not sorry to be gone
from her society. Something of her image,
cool as a peach on that hot afternoon, still
lingers in his memory: yet more of her conversation. 'You have there a very fine
parlour,' said the poor gentleman. — 'Ah,'
said Madame la Maréchale (des-logis), 'you
are very well acquainted with such parlours!'
And you should have seen with what a hard
and scornful eye she measured the vagabond
before her! I do not think he ever hated the
Commissary; but before that interview was at
an end, he hated Madame la Maréchale. His

passion (as I am led to understand by one who was present) stood confessed in a burning eye, a pale cheek, and a trembling utterance; Madame meanwhile tasting the joys of the matador, goading him with barbed words and staring him coldly down.

It was certainly good to be away from this lady, and better still to sit down to an excellent dinner in the inn. Here, too, the despised travellers scraped acquaintance with their next neighbour, a gentleman of these parts, returned from the day's sport, who had the good taste to find pleasure in their society. The dinner at an end, the gentleman proposed the acquaintance should be ripened in the café.

The café was crowded with sportsmen conclamantly explaining to each other and the world the smallness of their bags. About the centre of the room, the Cigarette and the Arethusa sat with their new acquaintance; a trio very well pleased, for the travellers (after their late experience) were greedy of consideration, and their sportsman rejoiced in a pair of patient listeners. Suddenly the glass door flew open with a crash; the Maréchal-des-logis appeared in the interval, gorgeously belted and befrogged, entered without salutation, strode up the room with a clang of spurs and weapons, and disappeared through a door at the far end. Close at his heels followed the Arethusa's gendarme of the afternoon, imitating, with a nice shade of difference, the imperial bearing of his chief; only, as he passed, he struck lightly with his open hand on the shoulder of his late captive, and with that ringing, dramatic utterance of which he had the secret—' *Suivez !* ' said he.

The arrest of the members, the oath of the Tennis Court, the signing of the declaration of independence, Mark Antony's oration, all the brave scenes of history, I conceive as having been not unlike that evening in the café at Châtillon. Terror breathed upon the assembly. A moment later, when the Arethusa had followed his recaptors into the farther part of the house, the Cigarette found himself alone with his coffee in a ring of empty chairs and tables, all the lusty sportsmen huddled into corners, all their clamorous voices hushed in whispering, all their eyes shooting at him furtively as at a leper.

And the Arethusa? Well, he had a long, sometimes a trying, interview in the back kitchen. The Maréchal-des-logis, who was a very handsome man, and I believe both intelligent and honest, had no clear opinion on the case. He thought the Commissary had done wrong, but he did not wish to get his subordinates into trouble; and he proposed this, that, and the other, to all of which the Arethusa (with a growing sense of his position) demurred.

'In short,' suggested the Arethusa, 'you want to wash your hands of further responsibility? Well, then, let me go to Paris.'

The Maréchal-des-logis looked at his watch.

'You may leave,' said he, 'by the ten o'clock train for Paris.'

And at noon the next day the travellers were telling their misadventure in the dining-room at Siron's.

V

RANDOM MEMORIES

I.—THE COAST OF FIFE

MANY writers have vigorously described the
pains of the first day or the first night at
school; to a boy of any enterprise, I believe,
they are more often agreeably exciting. Misery
—or at least misery unrelieved—is confined to
another period, to the days of suspense and the
'dreadful looking-for' of departure; when the
old life is running to an end, and the new life,
with its new interests, not yet begun; and to
the pain of an imminent parting, there is added
the unrest of a state of conscious pre-existence.
The area railings, the beloved shop-window,
the smell of semi-suburban tanpits, the song of
the church bells upon a Sunday, the thin, high
voices of compatriot children in a playing-field

—what a sudden, what an overpowering pathos breathes to him from each familiar circumstance! The assaults of sorrow come not from within, as it seems to him, but from without. I was proud and glad to go to school; had I been let alone, I could have borne up like any hero; but there was around me, in all my native town, a conspiracy of lamentation: 'Poor little boy, he is going away—unkind little boy, he is going to leave us'; so the unspoken burthen followed me as I went, with yearning and reproach. And at length, one melancholy afternoon in the early autumn, and at a place where it seems to me, looking back, it must be always autumn and generally Sunday, there came suddenly upon the face of all I saw—the long empty road, the lines of the tall houses, the church upon the hill, the woody hillside garden—a look of such a piercing sadness that my heart died; and seating myself on a door-step, I shed tears of miserable sympathy. A benevolent cat cumbered me the while with consolations— we two were alone in all that was visible of the London Road: two poor waifs who had

each tasted sorrow—and she fawned upon
the weeper, and gambolled for his entertainment, watching the effect, it seemed, with
motherly eyes.

For the sake of the cat, God bless her! I
confessed at home the story of my weakness;
and so it comes about that I owed a certain
journey, and the reader owes the present paper,
to a cat in the London Road. It was judged,
if I had thus brimmed over on the public highway, some change of scene was (in the medical
sense) indicated; my father at the time was
visiting the harbour lights of Scotland; and it
was decided he should take me along with him
around a portion of the shores of Fife; my first
professional tour, my first journey in the complete character of man, without the help of
petticoats.

The Kingdom of Fife (that royal province)
may be observed by the curious on the map,
occupying a tongue of land between the firths
of Forth and Tay. It may be continually seen
from many parts of Edinburgh (among the rest,
from the windows of my father's house) dying
away into the distance and the easterly *haar*

with one smoky seaside town beyond another, or in winter printing on the gray heaven some glittering hill-tops. It has no beauty to recommend it, being a low, sea-salted, wind-vexed promontory; trees very rare, except (as common on the east coast) along the dens of rivers; the fields well cultivated, I understand, but not lovely to the eye. It is of the coast I speak: the interior may be the garden of Eden. History broods over that part of the world like the easterly haar. Even on the map, its long row of Gaelic place-names bear testimony to an old and settled race. Of these little towns, posted along the shore as close as sedges, each with its bit of harbour, its old weather-beaten church or public building, its flavour of decayed prosperity and decaying fish, not one but has its legend, quaint or tragic : Dunfermline, in whose royal towers the king may be still observed (in the ballad) drinking the blood-red wine; somnolent Inverkeithing, once the quarantine of Leith; Aberdour, hard by the monastic islet of Inchcolm, hard by Donibristle where the 'bonny face was spoiled'; Burntisland where, when Paul Jones was off the coast, the Reverend

Mr. Shirra had a table carried between tide-
marks, and publicly prayed against the rover at
the pitch of his voice and his broad lowland
dialect; Kinghorn, where Alexander 'brak's
neckbane' and left Scotland to the English
wars; Kirkcaldy, where the witches once prevailed extremely and sank tall ships and honest
mariners in the North Sea; Dysart, famous—
well famous at least to me for the Dutch ships
that lay in its harbour, painted like toys and
with pots of flowers and cages of song-birds in
the cabin windows, and for one particular Dutch
skipper who would sit all day in slippers on the
break of the poop, smoking a long German
pipe; Wemyss (pronounce Weems) with its
bat-haunted caves, where the Chevalier John-
stone, on his flight from Culloden, passed a
night of superstitious terrors; Leven, a bald,
quite modern place, sacred to summer visitors,
whence there has gone but yesterday the tall
figure and the white locks of the last Englishman in Delhi, my uncle Dr. Balfour, who was
still walking his hospital rounds, while the
troopers from Meerut clattered and cried 'Deen
Deen' along the streets of the imperial city,

and Willoughby mustered his handful of heroes
at the magazine, and the nameless brave one in
the telegraph office was perhaps already fingering his last despatch; and just a little beyond
Leven, Largo Law and the smoke of Largo town
mounting about its feet, the town of Alexander
Selkirk, better known under the name of
Robinson Crusoe. So on, the list might be
pursued (only for private reasons, which the
reader will shortly have an opportunity to
guess) by St. Monance, and Pittenweem, and
the two Anstruthers, and Cellardyke, and Crail,
where Primate Sharpe was once a humble and
innocent country minister : on to the heel of
the land, to Fife Ness, overlooked by a sea-
wood of matted elders and the quaint old
mansion of Balcomie, itself overlooking but the
breach or the quiescence of the deep—the Carr
Rock beacon rising close in front, and as night
draws in, the star of the Inchcape reef spring-
ing up on the one hand, and the star of the
May Island on the other, and farther off yet a
third and a greater on the craggy foreland of
St. Abb's. And but a little way round the
corner of the land, imminent itself above the

sea, stands the gem of the province and the light of mediæval Scotland, St. Andrews, where the great Cardinal Beaton held garrison against the world, and the second of the name and title perished (as you may read in Knox's jeering narrative) under the knives of true-blue Protestants, and to this day (after so many centuries) the current voice of the professor is not hushed.

Here it was that my first tour of inspection began, early on a bleak easterly morning. There was a crashing run of sea upon the shore, I recollect, and my father and the man of the harbour light must sometimes raise their voices to be audible. Perhaps it is from this circumstance, that I always imagine St. Andrews to be an ineffectual seat of learning, and the sound of the east wind and the bursting surf to linger in its drowsy class-rooms and confound the utterance of the professor, until teacher and taught are alike drowned in oblivion, and only the sea-gull beats on the windows and the draught of the sea-air rustles in the pages of the open lecture. But upon all this, and the romance of St. Andrews in general, the reader must consult the works of Mr. Andrew Lang; who has written of it but the other day in his dainty prose and with his incommunicable humour, and long ago in one of his best poems, with grace, and local truth and a note of un-affected pathos. Mr. Lang knows all about the romance, I say, and the educational advan-tages, but I doubt if he had turned his attention to the harbour lights; and it may be news even to him, that in the year 1863 their case was pitiable. Hanging about with the east wind humming in my teeth, and my hands (I make no doubt) in my pockets, I looked for the first time upon that tragi-comedy of the visiting engineer which I have seen so often re-enacted on a more important stage. Eighty years ago, I find my grandfather writing: 'It is the most painful thing that can occur to me to have a correspondence of this kind with any of the keepers, and when I come to the Light House, instead of having the satisfaction to meet them with approbation and welcome their Family, it is distressing when one is obliged to put on a most angry countenance and demeanour.' This painful obligation has been hereditary in my

race. I have myself, on a perfectly amateur
and unauthorised inspection of Turnberry Point,
bent my brows upon the keeper on the question
of storm-panes; and felt a keen pang of self-
reproach, when we went down stairs again and
I found he was making a coffin for his infant
child; and then regained my equanimity with
the thought that I had done the man a service,
and when the proper inspector came, he would
be readier with his panes. The human race is
perhaps credited with more duplicity than it
deserves. The visitation of a lighthouse at
least is a business of the most transparent
nature. As soon as the boat grates on the
shore, and the keepers step forward in their
uniformed coats, the very slouch of the fellows'
shoulders tells their story, and the engineer may
begin at once to assume his 'angry countenance.' Certainly the brass of the handrail will
be clouded; and if the brass be not immaculate,
certainly all will be to match—the reflectors
scratched, the spare lamp unready, the storm-
panes in the storehouse. If a light is not
rather more than middling good, it will be
radically bad. Mediocrity (except in literature)

appears to be unattainable by man. But of course the unfortunate of St. Andrews was only an amateur, he was not in the Service, he had no uniform coat, he was (I believe) a plumber by his trade and stood (in the medi-æval phrase) quite out of the danger of my father; but he had a painful interview for all that, and perspired extremely.

From St. Andrews, we drove over Magus Muir. My father had announced we were 'to post,' and the phrase called up in my hopeful mind visions of top-boots and the pictures in Rowlandson's *Dance of Death;* but it was only a jingling cab that came to the inn door, such as I had driven in a thousand times at the low price of one shilling on the streets of Edin-burgh. Beyond this disappointment, I remem-ber nothing of that drive. It is a road I have often travelled, and of not one of these journeys do I remember any single trait. The fact has not been suffered to encroach on the truth of the imagination. I still see Magus Muir two hundred years ago; a desert place, quite un-inclosed; in the midst, the primate's carriage fleeing at the gallop; the assassins loose-reined

in pursuit, Burley Balfour, pistol in hand,
among the first. No scene of history has ever
written itself so deeply on my mind; not because Balfour, that questionable zealot, was an
ancestral cousin of my own; not because of
the pleadings of the victim and his daughter;
not even because of the live bum-bee that
flew out of Sharpe's 'bacco-box, thus clearly
indicating his complicity with Satan; nor
merely because, as it was after all a crime of
a fine religious flavour, it figured in Sunday
books and afforded a grateful relief from
Ministering Children or the *Memoirs of Mrs.
Katharine Winslowe*. The figure that always
fixed my attention is that of Hackston of
Rathillet, sitting in the saddle with his cloak
about his mouth, and through all that long,
bungling, vociferous hurly-burly, revolving privately a case of conscience. He would take
no hand in the deed, because he had a private
spite against the victim, and 'that action' must
be sullied with no suggestion of a worldly
motive; on the other hand, 'that action,' in
itself was highly justified, he had cast in his
lot with 'the actors,' and he must stay there,

inactive but publicly sharing the responsibility.
'You are a gentleman—you will protect me!'
cried the wounded old man, crawling towards
him. 'I will never lay a hand on you,' said
Hackston, and put his cloak about his mouth.
It is an old temptation with me, to pluck away
that cloak and see the face—to open that
bosom and to read the heart. With incomplete
romances about Hackston, the drawers of my
youth were lumbered. I read him up in every
printed book that I could lay my hands on.
I even dug among the Wodrow manuscripts,
sitting shame-faced in the very room where my
hero had been tortured two centuries before,
and keenly conscious of my youth in the midst
of other and (as I fondly thought) more gifted
students. All was vain: that he had passed a
riotous nonage, that he was a zealot, that he
twice displayed (compared with his grotesque
companions) some tincture of soldierly resolu-
tion and even of military common sense, and
that he figured memorably in the scene on
Magus Muir, so much and no more could
I make out. But whenever I cast my eyes
backward, it is to see him like a landmark on

the plains of history, sitting with his cloak about his mouth, inscrutable. How small a thing creates an immortality! I do not think he can have been a man entirely commonplace; but had he not thrown his cloak about his mouth, or had the witnesses forgot to chronicle the action, he would not thus have haunted the imagination of my boyhood, and to-day he would scarce delay me for a paragraph. An incident, at once romantic and dramatic, which at once awakes the judgment and makes a picture for the eye, how little do we realise its perdurable power! Perhaps no one does so but the author, just as none but he appreciates the influence of jingling words; so that he looks on upon life, with something of a covert smile, seeing people led by what they fancy to be thoughts and what are really the accustomed artifices of his own trade, or roused by what they take to be principles and are really picturesque effects. In a pleasant book about a school-class club, Colonel Fergusson has recently told a little anecdote. A 'Philosophical Society' was formed by some Academy boys—among them, Colonel Fergusson himself, Fleeming Jenkin, and Andrew Wilson, the Christian Buddhist and author of *The Abode of Snow*. Before these learned pundits, one member laid the following ingenious problem: 'What would be the result of putting a pound of potassium in a pot of porter?' 'I should think there would be a number of interesting bi-products,' said a smatterer at my elbow; but for me the tale itself has a bi-product, and stands as a type of much that is most human. For this inquirer who conceived himself to burn with a zeal entirely chemical, was really immersed in a design of a quite different nature; unconsciously to his own recently breeched intelligence, he was engaged in literature. Putting, pound, potassium, pot, porter; initial p, mediant t—that was his idea, poor little boy! So with politics and that which excites men in the present, so with history and that which rouses them in the past: there lie at the root of what appears, most serious unsuspected elements.

The triple town of Anstruther Wester, Anstruther Easter, and Cellardyke, all three

Royal Burghs—or two Royal Burghs and a less
distinguished suburb, I forget which—lies con-
tinuously along the seaside, and boasts of
either two or three separate parish churches,
and either two or three separate harbours.
These ambiguities are painful; but the fact is
(although it argue me uncultured), I am but
poorly posted upon Cellardyke. My business
lay in the two Anstruthers. A tricklet of a
stream divides them, spanned by a bridge; and
over the bridge at the time of my knowledge,
the celebrated Shell House stood outpost on
the west. This had been the residence of an
agreeable eccentric; during his fond tenancy,
he had illustrated the outer walls, as high (if I
remember rightly) as the roof, with elaborate
patterns and pictures, and snatches of verse in
the vein of *exegi monumentum;* shells and
pebbles, artfully contrasted and conjoined, had
been his medium; and I like to think of him
standing back upon the bridge, when all was
finished, drinking in the general effect and (like
Gibbon) already lamenting his employment.

The same bridge saw another sight in the
seventeenth century. Mr. Thomson, the 'curat'

of Anstruther Easter, was a man highly obnoxious to the devout: in the first place, because he was a 'curat'; in the second place, because he was a person of irregular and scandalous life; and in the third place, because he was generally suspected of dealings with the Enemy of Man. These three disqualifications, in the popular literature of the time, go hand in hand; but the end of Mr. Thomson was a thing quite by itself, and in the proper phrase, a manifest judgment. He had been at a friend's house in Anstruther Wester, where (and elsewhere, I suspect,) he had partaken of the bottle; indeed, to put the thing in our cold modern way, the reverend gentleman was on the brink of *delirium tremens*. It was a dark night, it seems; a little lassie came carrying a lantern to fetch the curate home; and away they went down the street of Anstruther Wester, the lantern swinging a bit in the child's hand, the barred lustre tossing up and down along the front of slumbering houses, and Mr. Thomson not altogether steady on his legs nor (to all appearance) easy in his mind. The pair had reached the middle of the bridge when (as I conceive the scene) the poor tippler started in some baseless fear and looked behind him; the child, already shaken by the minister's strange behaviour, started also; in so doing, she would jerk the lantern; and for the space of a moment the lights and the shadows would be all confounded. Then it was that to the unhinged toper and the twittering child, a huge bulk of blackness seemed to sweep down, to pass them close by as they stood upon the bridge, and to vanish on the farther side in the general darkness of the night. 'Plainly the devil come for Mr. Thomson!' thought the child. What Mr. Thomson thought himself, we have no ground of knowledge; but he fell upon his knees in the midst of the bridge like a man praying. On the rest of the journey to the manse, history is silent; but when they came to the door, the poor caitiff, taking the lantern from the child, looked upon her with so lost a countenance that her little courage died within her, and she fled home screaming to her parents. Not a soul would venture out; all that night, the minister dwelt alone with his terrors in the

manse; and when the day dawned, and men
made bold to go about the streets, they found
the devil had come indeed for Mr. Thomson.

This manse of Anstruther Easter has another
and a more cheerful association. It was early
in the morning, about a century before the days
of Mr. Thomson, that his predecessor was called
out of bed to welcome a Grandee of Spain, the
Duke of Medina Sidonia, just landed in the
harbour underneath. But sure there was never
seen a more decayed grandee; sure there was
never a duke welcomed from a stranger place
of exile. Half-way between Orkney and Shetland, there lies a certain isle; on the one hand
the Atlantic, on the other the North Sea,
bombard its pillared cliffs; sore-eyed, short-
living, inbred fishers and their families herd
in its few huts; in the graveyard pieces of
wreck-wood stand for monuments; there is
nowhere a more inhospitable spot. *Belle-Isle-
en-Mer*—Fair-Isle-at-Sea—that is a name that
has always rung in my mind's ear like music;
but the only 'Fair Isle' on which I ever set
my foot, was this unhomely, rugged turret-top
of submarine sierras. Here, when his ship

was broken, my lord Duke joyfully got ashore;
here for long months he and certain of his
men were harboured; and it was from this
durance that he landed at last to be welcomed
(as well as such a papist deserved, no doubt)
by the godly incumbent of Anstruther Easter;
and after the Fair Isle, what a fine city must
that have appeared! and after the island diet,
what a hospitable spot the minister's table!
And yet he must have lived on friendly terms
with his outlandish hosts. For to this day
there still survives a relic of the long winter
evenings when the sailors of the great Armada
crouched about the hearths of the Fair-Islanders,
the planks of their own lost galleon perhaps
lighting up the scene, and the gale and the
surf that beat about the coast contributing
their melancholy voices. All the folk of the
north isles are great artificers of knitting: the
Fair-Islanders alone dye their fabrics in the
Spanish manner. To this day, gloves and
nightcaps, innocently decorated, may be seen
for sale in the Shetland warehouse at Edin-
burgh, or on the Fair Isle itself in the catechist's

house; and to this day, they tell the story of
the Duke of Medina Sidonia's adventure.

It would seem as if the Fair Isle had some
attraction for 'persons of quality.' When I
landed there myself, an elderly gentleman,
unshaved, poorly attired, his shoulders wrapped
in a plaid, was seen walking to and fro, with a
book in his hand, upon the beach. He paid
no heed to our arrival, which we thought a
strange thing in itself; but when one of the
officers of the *Pharos*, passing narrowly by
him, observed his book to be a Greek Testament, our wonder and interest took a higher
flight. The catechist was cross-examined; he
said the gentleman had been put across some
time before in Mr. Bruce of Sumburgh's schooner,
the only link between the Fair Isle and the rest
of the world; and that he held services and was
doing 'good.' So much came glibly enough;
but when pressed a little farther, the catechist
displayed embarrassment. A singular diffidence
appeared upon his face: 'They tell me,' said he,
in low tones, 'that he's a lord.' And a lord he
was; a peer of the realm pacing that inhospi-

table beach with his Greek Testament, and his plaid about his shoulders, set upon doing good, as he understood it, worthy man! And his grandson, a good-looking little boy, much better dressed than the lordly evangelist, and speaking with a silken English accent very foreign to the scene, accompanied me for a while in my exploration of the island. I suppose this little fellow is now my lord, and wonder how much he remembers of the Fair Isle. Perhaps not much; for he seemed to accept very quietly his savage situation; and under such guidance, it is like that this was not his first nor yet his last adventure.

VI

RANDOM MEMORIES

II. — THE EDUCATION OF AN ENGINEER

ANSTRUTHER is a place sacred to the Muse: she inspired (really to a considerable extent) Tennant's vernacular poem *Anst'er Fair;* and I have there waited upon her myself with much devotion. This was when I came as a young man to glean engineering experience from the building of the breakwater. What I gleaned, I am sure I do not know; but indeed I had already my own private determination to be an author; I loved the art of words and the appearances of life; and *travellers*, and *headers*, and *rubble*, and *polished ashlar*, and *pierres perdues*, and even the thrilling question of the *string-course*, interested me only (if they interested me at all) as properties for some possible romance or as words to add to my vocabulary. To grow a little catholic is the compensation of years; youth is one-eyed; and in those days, though I haunted the breakwater by day, and even loved the place for the sake of the sunshine, the thrilling seaside air, the wash of waves on the sea-face, the green glimmer of the divers' helmets far below, and the musical chinking of the masons, my one genuine preoccupation lay elsewhere, and my only industry was in the hours when I was not on duty. I lodged with a certain Bailie Brown, a carpenter by trade; and there, as soon as dinner was despatched, in a chamber scented with dry rose-leaves, drew in my chair to the table and proceeded to pour forth literature, at such a speed, and with such intimations of early death and immortality, as I now look back upon with wonder. Then it was that I wrote *Voces Fidelium*, a series of dramatic monologues in verse; then that I indited the bulk of a covenanting novel — like so many others, never finished. Late I sat into the night, toiling (as I thought) under the very dart of death, toiling to leave a memory behind me. I feel moved to thrust

aside the curtain of the years, to hail that poor
feverish idiot, to bid him go to bed and clap
Voces Fidelium on the fire before he goes; so
clear does he appear before me, sitting there
between his candles in the rose-scented room
and the late night; so ridiculous a picture (to
my elderly wisdom) does the fool present! But
he was driven to his bed at last without
miraculous intervention; and the manner of his
driving sets the last touch upon this eminently
youthful business. The weather was then so
warm that I must keep the windows open; the
night without was populous with moths. As
the late darkness deepened, my literary tapers
beaconed forth more brightly; thicker and
thicker came the dusty night-fliers, to gyrate
for one brilliant instant round the flame and
fall in agonies upon my paper. Flesh and blood
could not endure the spectacle; to capture immortality was doubtless a noble enterprise, but
not to capture it at such a cost of suffering; and
out would go the candles, and off would I go
to bed in the darkness, raging to think that
the blow might fall on the morrow, and there
was *Voces Fidelium* still incomplete. Well, the

moths are all gone, and *Voces Fidelium* along
with them; only the fool is still on hand and
practises new follies.

Only one thing in connection with the harbour tempted me, and that was the diving, an
experience I burned to taste of. But this was
not to be, at least in Anstruther; and the subject involves a change of scene to the sub-arctic
town of Wick. You can never have dwelt in
a country more unsightly than that part of
Caithness, the land faintly swelling, faintly
falling, not a tree, not a hedgerow, the fields
divided by single slate stones set upon their
edge, the wind always singing in your ears and
(down the long road that led nowhere) thrum-
ming in the telegraph wires. Only as you
approached the coast was there anything to stir
the heart. The plateau broke down to the
North Sea in formidable cliffs, the tall out-stacks
rose like pillars ringed about with surf, the coves
were over-brimmed with clamorous froth, the
sea-birds screamed, the wind sang in the thyme
on the cliff's edge; here and there, small ancient
castles toppled on the brim; here and there, it
was possible to dip into a dell of shelter, where

you might lie and tell yourself you were a little
warm, and hear (near at hand) the whin-pods
bursting in the afternoon sun, and (farther off)
the rumour of the turbulent sea.   As for Wick
itself, it is one of the meanest of man's towns,
and situate certainly on the baldest of God's
bays.   It lives for herring, and a strange sight
it is to see (of an afternoon) the heights of
Pulteney blackened by seaward-looking fishers,
as when a city crowds to a review—or, as when
bees have swarmed, the ground is horrible with
lumps and clusters; and a strange sight, and a
beautiful, to see the fleet put silently out against
a rising moon, the sea-line rough as a wood with
sails, and ever and again and one after another,
a boat flitting swiftly by the silver disk.   This
mass of fishers, this great fleet of boats, is out
of all proportion to the town itself; and the
oars are manned and the nets hauled by immi-
grants from the Long Island (as we call the
outer Hebrides), who come for that season only,
and depart again, if 'the take' be poor, leaving
debts behind them.   In a bad year, the end of
the herring fishery is therefore an exciting
time; fights are common, riots often possible;

an apple knocked from a child's hand was once
the signal for something like a war; and even
when I was there, a gunboat lay in the bay to
assist the authorities. To contrary interests, it
should be observed, the curse of Babel is here
added; the Lews men are Gaelic speakers.
Caithness has adopted English; an odd circumstance, if you reflect that both must be largely
Norsemen by descent. I remember seeing one
of the strongest instances of this division: a
thing like a Punch-and-Judy box erected on
the flat grave-stones of the churchyard; from
the hutch or proscenium—I know not what to
call it—an eldritch-looking preacher laying down
the law in Gaelic about some one of the name
of *Powl*, whom I at last divined to be the apostle
to the Gentiles; a large congregation of the
Lews men very devoutly listening; and on the
outskirts of the crowd, some of the town's
children (to whom the whole affair was Greek
and Hebrew) profanely playing tigg. The
same descent, the same country, the same narrow sect of the same religion, and all these
bonds made very largely nugatory by an acci-
dental difference of dialect!

Into the bay of Wick stretched the dark length of the unfinished breakwater, in its cage of open staging; the travellers (like frames of churches) over-plumbing all; and away at the extreme end, the divers toiling unseen on the foundation. On a platform of loose planks, the assistants turned their air-mills; a stone might be swinging between wind and water; underneath the swell ran gaily; and from time to time, a mailed dragon with a window-glass snout came dripping up the ladder. Youth is a blessed season after all; my stay at Wick was in the year of *Voces Fidelium* and the rose-leaf room at Bailie Brown's; and already I did not care two straws for literary glory. Posthumous ambition perhaps requires an atmosphere of roses; and the more rugged excitant of Wick east winds had made another boy of me. To go down in the diving-dress, that was my absorbing fancy; and with the countenance of a certain handsome scamp of a diver, Bob Bain by name, I gratified the whim.

It was gray, harsh, easterly weather, the swell ran pretty high, and out in the open there were 'skipper's daughters,' when I found

myself at last on the diver's platform, twenty
pounds of lead upon each foot and my whole
person swollen with ply and ply of woollen
underclothing. One moment, the salt wind
was whistling round my night-capped head;
the next, I was crushed almost double under
the weight of the helmet. As that intolerable
burthen was laid upon me, I could have found
it in my heart (only for shame's sake) to cry
off from the whole enterprise. But it was too
late. The attendants began to turn the hurdy-
gurdy, and the air to whistle through the tube;
some one screwed in the barred window of the
vizor; and I was cut off in a moment from my
fellow-men; standing there in their midst, but
quite divorced from intercourse: a creature
deaf and dumb, pathetically looking forth upon
them from a climate of his own. Except that
I could move and feel, I was like a man fallen
in a catalepsy. But time was scarce given me
to realise my isolation; the weights were hung
upon my back and breast, the signal rope was
thrust into my unresisting hand; and setting a
twenty-pound foot upon the ladder, I began
ponderously to descend.

Some twenty rounds below the platform, twilight fell. Looking up, I saw a low green heaven mottled with vanishing bells of white; looking around, except for the weedy spokes and shafts of the ladder, nothing but a green gloaming, somewhat opaque but very restful and delicious. Thirty rounds lower, I stepped off on the *pierres perdues* of the foundation; a dumb helmeted figure took me by the hand, and made a gesture (as I read it) of encouragement; and looking in at the creature's window, I beheld the face of Bain. There we were, hand to hand and (when it pleased us) eye to eye; and either might have burst himself with shouting, and not a whisper come to his companion's hearing. Each, in his own little world of air, stood incommunicably separate.

Bob had told me ere this a little tale, a five minutes' drama at the bottom of the sea, which at that moment possibly shot across my mind. He was down with another, settling a stone of the sea-wall. They had it well adjusted, Bob gave the signal, the scissors were slipped, the stone set home; and it was time to turn to something else. But still his companion remained bowed over the block like a mourner on a tomb, or only raised himself to make absurd contortions and mysterious signs unknown to the vocabulary of the diver. There, then, these two stood for awhile, like the dead and the living; till there flashed a fortunate thought into Bob's mind, and he stooped, peered through the window of that other world, and beheld the face of its inhabitant wet with streaming tears. Ah! the man was in pain! And Bob, glancing downward, saw what was the trouble: the block had been lowered on the foot of that unfortunate—he was caught alive at the bottom of the sea under fifteen tons of rock.

That two men should handle a stone so heavy, even swinging in the scissors, may appear strange to the inexpert. These must bear in mind the great density of the water of the sea, and the surprising results of transplantation to that medium. To understand a little what these are, and how a man's weight, so far from being an encumbrance, is the very ground of his agility, was the chief lesson of my submarine experience. The knowledge came upon

me by degrees. As I began to go forward
with the hand of my estranged companion, a
world of tumbled stones was visible, pillared
with the weedy uprights of the staging: overhead, a flat roof of green: a little in front, the
sea-wall, like an unfinished rampart. And presently in our upward progress, Bob motioned me
to leap upon a stone; I looked to see if he were
possibly in earnest, and he only signed to me
the more imperiously. Now the block stood
six feet high; it would have been quite a leap
to me unencumbered; with the breast and
back weights, and the twenty pounds upon
each foot, and the staggering load of the helmet, the thing was out of reason. I laughed
aloud in my tomb; and to prove to Bob how
far he was astray, I gave a little impulse from
my toes. Up I soared like a bird, my companion soaring at my side. As high as to the stone,
and then higher, I pursued my impotent and
empty flight. Even when the strong arm of
Bob had checked my shoulders, my heels continued their ascent; so that I blew out side-
ways like an autumn leaf, and must be hauled
in, hand over hand, as sailors haul in the slack

of a sail, and propped upon my feet again like an intoxicated sparrow. Yet a little higher on the foundation, and we began to be affected by the bottom of the swell, running there like a strong breeze of wind. Or so I must suppose; for, safe in my cushion of air, I was conscious of no impact; only swayed idly like a weed, and was now borne helplessly abroad, and now swiftly —and yet with dream-like gentleness—impelled against my guide. So does a child's balloon divagate upon the currents of the air, and touch and slide off again from every obstacle. So must have ineffectually swung, so resented their inefficiency, those light crowds that followed the Star of Hades, and uttered exiguous voices in the land beyond Cocytus.

There was something strangely exasperating, as well as strangely wearying, in these uncommanded evolutions. It is bitter to return to infancy, to be supported, and directed, and perpetually set upon your feet, by the hand of someone else. The air besides, as it is supplied to you by the busy millers on the platform, closes the eustachian tubes and keeps the neophyte perpetually swallowing, till his throat is grown so dry that he can swallow no longer. And for all these reasons—although I had a fine, dizzy, muddle-headed joy in my surroundings, and longed, and tried, and always failed, to lay hands on the fish that darted here and there about me, swift as humming-birds— yet I fancy I was rather relieved than otherwise when Bain brought me back to the ladder and signed to me to mount. And there was one more experience before me even then. Of a sudden, my ascending head passed into the trough of a swell. Out of the green, I shot at once into a glory of rosy, almost of sanguine light—the multitudinous seas incarnadined, the heaven above a vault of crimson. And then the glory faded into the hard, ugly daylight of a Caithness autumn, with a low sky, a gray sea, and a whistling wind.

Bob Bain had five shillings for his trouble, and I had done what I desired. It was one of the best things I got from my education as an engineer: of which however, as a way of life, I wish to speak with sympathy. It takes a man into the open air; it keeps him hanging about harbour-sides, which is the richest form of idling;

it carries him to wild islands; it gives him a
taste of the genial dangers of the sea; it
supplies him with dexterities to exercise; it
makes demands upon his ingenuity; it will go
far to cure him of any taste (if ever he had one)
for the miserable life of cities.   And when it
has done so, it carries him back and shuts him
in an office!   From the roaring skerry and the
wet thwart of the tossing boat, he passes to the
stool and desk; and with a memory full of
ships, and seas, and perilous headlands, and the
shining pharos, he must apply his long-sighted
eyes to the petty niceties of drawing, or measure
his inaccurate mind with several pages of con-
secutive figures.   He is a wise youth, to be
sure, who can balance one part of genuine life
against two parts of drudgery between four
walls, and for the sake of the one, manfully
accept the other.

Wick was scarce an eligible place of stay.
But how much better it was to hang in the cold
wind upon the pier, to go down with Bob Bain
among the roots of the staging, to be all day in
a boat coiling a wet rope and shouting orders
—not always very wise—than to be warm and

dry, and dull, and dead-alive, in the most comfortable office. And Wick itself had in those days a note of originality. It may have still, but I misdoubt it much. The old minister of Keiss would not preach, in these degenerate times, for an hour and a half upon the clock. The gipsies must be gone from their caverns; where you might see, from the mouth, the women tending their fire, like Meg Merrilies, and the men sleeping off their coarse potations; and where in winter gales, the surf would beleaguer them closely, bursting in their very door. A traveller to-day upon the Thurso coach would scarce observe a little cloud of smoke among the moorlands, and be told, quite openly, it marked a private still. He would not indeed make that journey, for there is now no Thurso coach. And even if he could, one little thing that happened to me could never happen to him, or not with the same trenchancy of contrast.

We had been upon the road all evening; the coach-top was crowded with Lews fishers going home, scarce anything but Gaelic had sounded in my ears; and our way had lain throughout over a moorish country very northern to behold. Latish at night, though it was still broad day in our subarctic latitude, we came down upon the shores of the roaring Pentland Firth, that grave of mariners ; on one hand, the cliffs of Dunnet Head ran seaward ; in front was the little bare, white town of Castleton, its streets full of blowing sand ; nothing beyond, but the North Islands, the great deep, and the perennial ice-fields of the Pole.   And here, in the last imaginable place, there sprang up young outlandish voices and a chatter of some foreign speech ; and I saw, pursuing the coach with its load of Hebridean fishers—as they had pursued *vetturini* up the passes of the Apennines or perhaps along the grotto under Virgil's tomb — two little dark-eyed, white-toothed Italian vagabonds, of twelve to fourteen years of age, one with a hurdy-gurdy, the other with a cage of white mice.   The coach passed on, and their small Italian chatter died in the distance ; and I was left to marvel how they had wandered into that country, and how they fared in it, and what they thought of it, and when (if ever) they should see again the silver wind-breaks run among the olives, and the stone-pine stand guard upon Etruscan sepulchres.

Upon any American, the strangeness of this incident is somewhat lost. For as far back as he goes in his own land, he will find some alien camping there; the Cornish miner, the French or Mexican half-blood, the negro in the South, these are deep in the woods and far among the mountains. But in an old, cold, and rugged country such as mine, the days of immigration are long at an end; and away up there, which was at that time far beyond the northernmost extreme of railways, hard upon the shore of that ill-omened strait of whirlpools, in a land of moors where no stranger came, unless it should be a sportsman to shoot grouse or an antiquary to decipher runes, the presence of these small pedestrians struck the mind as though a bird-of-paradise had risen from the heather or an albatross come fishing in the bay of Wick. They were as strange to their surroundings as my lordly evangelist or the old Spanish grandee on the Fair Isle.

VII

THE LANTERN–BEARERS

I

THESE boys congregated every autumn about a certain easterly fisher-village, where they tasted in a high degree the glory of existence. The place was created seemingly on purpose for the diversion of young gentlemen. A street or two of houses, mostly red and many of them tiled; a number of fine trees clustered about the manse and the kirkyard, and turning the chief street into a shady alley; many little gardens more than usually bright with flowers; nets a-drying, and fisher-wives scolding in the backward parts; a smell of fish, a genial smell of seaweed; whiffs of blowing sand at the street-corners; shops with golf-balls and bottled lollipops; another shop with penny pickwicks (that re-

markable cigar) and the *London Journal*, dear
to me for its startling pictures, and a few
novels, dear for their suggestive names: such,
as well as memory serves me, were the ingredients of the town. These, you are to conceive
posted on a spit between two sandy bays, and
sparsely flanked with villas—enough for the
boys to lodge in with their subsidiary parents,
not enough (not yet enough) to cocknify the
scene: a haven in the rocks in front: in front
of that, a file of gray islets: to the left, endless
links and sand wreaths, a wilderness of hiding-
holes, alive with popping rabbits and soaring
gulls: to the right, a range of seaward crags,
one rugged brow beyond another; the ruins of
a mighty and ancient fortress on the brink of
one; coves between—now charmed into sunshine quiet, now whistling with wind and
clamorous with bursting surges; the dens and
sheltered hollows redolent of thyme and south-
ernwood, the air at the cliff's edge brisk and
clean and pungent of the sea—in front of all,
the Bass Rock, tilted seaward like a doubtful
bather, the surf ringing it with white, the solan-
geese hanging round its summit like a great

and glittering smoke. This choice piece of seaboard was sacred, besides, to the wrecker; and the Bass, in the eye of fancy, still flew the colours of King James; and in the ear of fancy the arches of Tantallon still rang with horse-shoe iron, and echoed to the commands of Bell-the-Cat.

There was nothing to mar your days, if you were a boy summering in that part, but the embarrassment of pleasure. You might golf if you wanted; but I seem to have been better employed. You might secrete yourself in the Lady's Walk, a certain sunless dingle of elders, all mossed over by the damp as green as grass, and dotted here and there by the streamside with roofless walls, the cold homes of anchorites. To fit themselves for life, and with a special eye to acquire the art of smoking, it was even common for the boys to harbour there; and you might have seen a single penny pickwick, honestly shared in lengths with a blunt knife, bestrew the glen with these apprentices. Again, you might join our fishing parties, where we sat perched as thick as solan-geese, a covey of little anglers, boy and girl, angling over each

other's heads, to the much entanglement of
lines and loss of podleys and consequent shrill
recrimination—shrill as the geese themselves.
Indeed, had that been all, you might have done
this often; but though fishing be a fine pastime, the podley is scarce to be regarded as
a dainty for the table; and it was a point of
honour that a boy should eat all that he had
taken. Or again, you might climb the Law,
where the whale's jawbone stood landmark in
the buzzing wind, and behold the face of many
counties, and the smoke and spires of many
towns, and the sails of distant ships. You
might bathe, now in the flaws of fine weather,
that we pathetically call our summer, now in a
gale of wind, with the sand scourging your bare
hide, your clothes thrashing abroad from underneath their guardian stone, the froth of the
great breakers casting you headlong ere it had
drowned your knees. Or you might explore
the tidal rocks, above all in the ebb of springs,
when the very roots of the hills were for the
nonce discovered; following my leader from
one group to another, groping in slippery tangle
for the wreck of ships, wading in pools after the

abominable creatures of the sea, and ever with
an eye cast backward on the march of the tide
and the menaced line of your retreat.   And
then you might go Crusoeing, a word that
covers all extempore eating in the open air:
digging perhaps a house under the margin of
the links, kindling a fire of the sea-ware, and
cooking apples there—if they were truly apples,
for I sometimes suppose the merchant must
have played us off with some inferior and quite
local fruit, capable of resolving, in the neighbourhood of fire, into mere sand and smoke
and iodine; or perhaps pushing to Tantallon,
you might lunch on sandwiches and visions in
the grassy court, while the wind hummed in the
crumbling turrets; or clambering along the
coast, eat geans [1] (the worst, I must suppose, in
Christendom) from an adventurous gean tree
that had taken root under a cliff, where it was
shaken with an ague of east wind, and silvered
after gales with salt, and grew so foreign among
its bleak surroundings that to eat of its produce
was an adventure in itself.

There are mingled some dismal memories

[1] Wild cherries.

with so many that were joyous. Of the fisher-wife, for instance, who had cut her throat at Canty Bay; and of how I ran with the other children to the top of the Quadrant, and beheld a posse of silent people escorting a cart, and on the cart, bound in a chair, her throat bandaged, and the bandage all bloody—horror!—the fisher-wife herself, who continued thenceforth to hag-ride my thoughts, and even to-day (as I recall the scene) darkens daylight. She was lodged in the little old jail in the chief street; but whether or no she died there, with a wise terror of the worst, I never inquired. She had been tippling; it was but a dingy tragedy; and it seems strange and hard that, after all these years, the poor crazy sinner should be still pilloried on her cart in the scrap-book of my memory. Nor shall I readily forget a certain house in the Quadrant where a visitor died, and a dark old woman continued to dwell alone with the dead body; nor how this old woman conceived a hatred to myself and one of my cousins, and in the dread hour of the dusk, as we were clambering on the garden-walls, opened a window in that house of mortality and cursed

us in a shrill voice and with a marrowy choice
of language. It was a pair of very colourless
urchins that fled down the lane from this
remarkable experience! But I recall with a
more doubtful sentiment, compounded out of
fear and exultation, the coil of equinoctial
tempests; trumpeting squalls, scouring flaws of
rain ; the boats with their reefed lugsails
scudding for the harbour mouth, where danger
lay, for it was hard to make when the wind
had any east in it; the wives clustered with
blowing shawls at the pier-head, where (if fate
was against them) they might see boat and
husband and sons—their whole wealth and
their whole family—engulfed under their eyes;
and (what I saw but once) a troop of neighbours
forcing such an unfortunate homeward, and she
squalling and battling in their midst, a figure
scarcely human, a tragic Mænad.

These are things that I recall with interest;
but what my memory dwells upon the most, I
have been all this while withholding. It was a
sport peculiar to the place, and indeed to a
week or so of our two months' holiday there.
Maybe it still flourishes in its native spot; for

boys and their pastimes are swayed by periodic forces inscrutable to man; so that tops and marbles reappear in their due season, regular like the sun and moon; and the harmless art of knucklebones has seen the fall of the Roman empire and the rise of the United States. It may still flourish in its native spot, but nowhere else, I am persuaded; for I tried myself to introduce it on Tweedside, and was defeated lamentably; its charm being quite local, like a country wine that cannot be exported.

The idle manner of it was this :—

Toward the end of September, when school-time was drawing near and the nights were already black, we would begin to sally from our respective villas, each equipped with a tin bull's-eye lantern. The thing was so well known that it had worn a rut in the commerce of Great Britain; and the grocers, about the due time, began to garnish their windows with our particular brand of luminary. We wore them buckled to the waist upon a cricket belt, and over them, such was the rigour of the game, a buttoned top-coat. They smelled noisomely of blistered tin; they never burned aright, though

they would always burn our fingers; their use
was naught; the pleasure of them merely fanci-
ful; and yet a boy with a bull's-eye under his
top-coat asked for nothing more. The fishermen used lanterns about their boats, and it was
from them, I suppose, that we had got the
hint; but theirs were not bull's-eyes, nor did we
ever play at being fishermen. The police
carried them at their belts, and we had plainly
copied them in that; yet we did not pretend to
be policemen. Burglars, indeed, we may have
had some haunting thoughts of; and we had
certainly an eye to past ages when lanterns
were more common, and to certain story-books
in which we had found them to figure very
largely. But take it for all in all, the pleasure
of the thing was substantive; and to be a boy
with a bull's-eye under his top-coat was good
enough for us.

When two of these asses met, there would
be an anxious 'Have you got your lantern?'
and a gratified 'Yes!' That was the shibbo-
leth, and very needful too; for, as it was the
rule to keep our glory contained, none could

recognise a lantern-bearer, unless (like the pole-cat) by the smell. Four or five would sometimes climb into the belly of a ten-man lugger, with nothing but the thwarts above them—for the cabin was usually locked, or choose out some hollow of the links where the wind might whistle overhead. There the coats would be unbuttoned and the bull's-eyes discovered; and in the chequering glimmer, under the huge windy hall of the night, and cheered by a rich steam of toasting tinware, these fortunate young gentlemen would crouch together in the cold sand of the links or on the scaly bilges of the fishing-boat, and delight themselves with inappropriate talk. Woe is me that I may not give some specimens— some of their foresights of life, or deep in- quiries into the rudiments of man and nature, these were so fiery and so innocent, they were so richly silly, so romantically young. But the talk, at any rate, was but a condiment; and these gatherings themselves only accidents in the career of the lantern-bearer. The essence of this bliss was to walk by yourself in the black night; the slide shut, the top-coat buttoned; not a ray escaping, whether to conduct your footsteps or to make your glory public : a mere pillar of darkness in the dark ; and all the while, deep down in the privacy of your fool's heart, to know you had a bull's-eye at your belt, and to exult and sing over the knowledge.

II

It is said that a poet has died young in the breast of the most stolid. It may be contended, rather, that this (somewhat minor) bard in almost every case survives, and is the spice of life to his possessor. Justice is not done to the versatility and the unplumbed childishness of man's imagination. His life from without may seem but a rude mound of mud; there will be some golden chamber at the heart of it, in which he dwells delighted; and for as dark as his pathway seems to the observer, he will have some kind of a bull's-eye at his belt.

It would be hard to pick out a career more

cheerless than that of Dancer, the miser, as he figures in the 'Old Bailey Reports,' a prey to the most sordid persecutions, the butt of his neighbourhood, betrayed by his hired man, his house beleaguered by the impish school-boy, and he himself grinding and fuming and impotently fleeing to the law against these pin-pricks. You marvel at first that any one should willingly prolong a life so destitute of charm and dignity; and then you call to memory that had he chosen, had he ceased to be a miser, he could have been freed at once from these trials, and might have built himself a castle and gone escorted by a squadron. For the love of more recondite joys, which we cannot estimate, which, it may be, we should envy, the man had willingly foregone both comfort and consideration. 'His mind to him a kingdom was'; and sure enough, digging into that mind, which seems at first a dust-heap, we unearth some priceless jewels. For Dancer must have had the love of power and the disdain of using it, a noble character in itself; disdain of many pleasures, a chief part of what is commonly called wisdom; disdain of the inevitable end, that finest trait of mankind; scorn of men's opinions, another element of virtue; and at the back of all, a conscience just like yours and mine, whining like a cur, swindling like a thimble-rigger, but still pointing (there or thereabout) to some conventional standard. Here were a cabinet portrait to which Hawthorne perhaps had done justice; and yet not Hawthorne either, for he was mildly minded, and it lay not in him to create for us that throb of the miser's pulse, his fretful energy of gusto, his vast arms of ambition clutching in he knows not what: insatiable, insane, a god with a muck-rake. Thus, at least, looking in the bosom of the miser, consideration detects the poet in the full tide of life, with more, indeed, of the poetic fire than usually goes to epics; and tracing that mean man about his cold hearth, and to and fro in his discomfortable house, spies within him a blazing bonfire of delight. And so with others, who do not live by bread alone, but by some cherished and perhaps fantastic pleasure; who are meat salesmen to the external eye, and possibly to themselves are Shakespeares, Napoleons, or Beethovens; who have not one virtue to rub against another in the field of active life, and yet perhaps, in the life of contemplation, sit with the saints. We see them on the street, and we can count their buttons; but heaven knows in what they pride themselves! heaven knows where they have set their treasure!

There is one fable that touches very near the quick of life: the fable of the monk who passed into the woods, heard a bird break into song, hearkened for a trill or two, and found himself on his return a stranger at his convent gates; for he had been absent fifty years, and of all his comrades there survived but one to recognise him. It is not only in the woods that this enchanter carols, though perhaps he is native there. He sings in the most doleful places. The miser hears him and chuckles, and the days are moments. With no more apparatus than an ill-smelling lantern I have evoked him on the naked links. All life that is not merely mechanical is spun out of two strands: seeking for that bird and hearing him. And it is just this that makes life so hard to value, and the delight of each so incommunicable. And just a knowledge of this, and a remembrance of those fortunate hours in which the bird has sung to us, that fills us with such wonder when we turn the pages of the realist. There, to be sure, we find a picture of life in so far as it consists of mud and of old iron, cheap desires and cheap fears, that which we are ashamed to remember and that which we are careless whether we forget; but of the note of that time-devouring nightingale we hear no news.

The case of these writers of romance is most obscure. They have been boys and youths; they have lingered outside the window of the beloved, who was then most probably writing to some one else; they have sat before a sheet of paper, and felt themselves mere continents of congested poetry, not one line of which would flow; they have walked alone in the woods, they have walked in cities under the countless lamps; they have been to sea, they have hated, they have feared, they have longed to knife a man, and maybe done it; the wild taste of life has stung their palate. Or, if you deny them all the rest, one pleasure at least they have tasted to the full—their books are there to prove it—the keen pleasure of successful literary composition. And yet they fill the globe with volumes, whose cleverness inspires me with despairing admiration, and whose consistent falsity to all I care to call existence, with despairing wrath. If I had no better hope than to continue to revolve among the dreary and petty businesses, and to be moved by the paltry hopes and fears with which they surround and animate their heroes, I declare I would die now. But there has never an hour of mine gone quite so dully yet; if it were spent waiting at a railway junction, I would have some scattering thoughts, I could count some grains of memory, compared to which the whole of one of these romances seems but dross.

These writers would retort (if I take them properly) that this was very true; that it was the same with themselves and other persons of (what they call) the artistic temperament; that in this we were exceptional, and should apparently be ashamed of ourselves; but that our works must deal exclusively with (what they call) the average man, who was a prodigious dull fellow, and quite dead to all but the paltriest considerations. I accept the issue. We can only know others by ourselves. The artistic temperament (a plague on the expression!) does not make us different from our fellow-men, or it would make us incapable of writing novels; and the average man (a murrain on the word!) is just like you and me, or he would not be average. It was Whitman who stamped a kind of Birmingham sacredness upon the latter phrase; but Whitman knew very well, and showed very nobly, that the average man was full of joys and full of a poetry of his own. And this harping on life's dulness and man's meanness is a loud profession of incompetence; it is one of two things: the cry of the blind eye, *I cannot see*, or the complaint of the dumb tongue, *I cannot utter.* To draw a life without delights is to prove I have not realised it. To picture a man without some sort of poetry—well, it goes near to prove my case, for it shows an author may have little enough. To see Dancer only as a

dirty, old, small-minded, impotently fuming
man, in a dirty house, besieged by Harrow
boys, and probably beset by small attorneys,
is to show myself as keen an observer as
. . . the Harrow boys. But these young
gentlemen (with a more becoming modesty)
were content to pluck Dancer by the coat-
tails; they did not suppose they had surprised
his secret or could put him living in a book:
and it is there my error would have lain.
Or say that in the same romance—I continue
to call these books romances, in the hope of
giving pain—say that in the same romance,
which now begins really to take shape, I should
leave to speak of Dancer, and follow instead
the Harrow boys; and say that I came on
some such business as that of my lantern-
bearers on the links; and described the boys
as very cold, spat upon by flurries of rain,
and drearily surrounded, all of which they
were; and their talk as silly and indecent,
which it certainly was. I might upon these
lines, and had I Zola's genius, turn out, in a
page or so, a gem of literary art, render the
lantern-light with the touches of a master,

and lay on the indecency with the ungrudging hand of love; and when all was done, what a triumph would my picture be of shallowness and dulness! how it would have missed the point! how it would have belied the boys! To the ear of the stenographer, the talk is merely silly and indecent; but ask the boys themselves, and they are discussing (as it is highly proper they should) the possibilities of existence. To the eye of the observer they are wet and cold and drearily surrounded; but ask themselves, and they are in the heaven of a recondite pleasure, the ground of which is an ill-smelling lantern.

III

For, to repeat, the ground of a man's joy is often hard to hit. It may hinge at times upon a mere accessory, like the lantern, it may reside, like Dancer's, in the mysterious inwards of psychology. It may consist with perpetual failure, and find exercise in the continued chase. It has so little bond with externals (such as the observer scribbles in his

note-book) that it may even touch them not;
and the man's true life, for which he consents
to live, lie altogether in the field of fancy. The
clergyman, in his spare hours, may be winning
battles, the farmer sailing ships, the banker
reaping triumph in the arts: all leading another life, plying another trade from that they
chose; like the poet's housebuilder, who, after
all is cased in stone,

> ' By his fireside, as impotent fancy prompts,
> Rebuilds it to his liking.'

In such a case the poetry runs underground.
The observer (poor soul, with his documents!)
is all abroad. For to look at the man is
but to court deception. We shall see the
trunk from which he draws his nourishment;
but he himself is above and abroad in the green
dome of foliage, hummed through by winds
and nested in by nightingales. And the true
realism were that of the poets, to climb up
after him like a squirrel, and catch some
glimpse of the heaven for which he lives.
And the true realism, always and everywhere,
is that of the poets: to find out where

joy resides, and give it a voice far beyond singing.

For to miss the joy is to miss all. In the joy of the actors lies the sense of any action. That is the explanation, that the excuse. To one who has not the secret of the lanterns, the scene upon the links is meaningless. And hence the haunting and truly spectral unreality of realistic books. Hence, when we read the English realists, the incredulous wonder with which we observe the hero's constancy under the submerging tide of dulness, and how he bears up with his jibbing sweetheart, and endures the chatter of idiot girls, and stands by his whole unfeatured wilderness of an existence, instead of seeking relief in drink or foreign travel. Hence in the French, in that meat-market of middle-aged sensuality, the disgusted surprise with which we see the hero drift sidelong, and practically quite untempted, into every description of misconduct and dishonour. In each, we miss the personal poetry, the enchanted atmosphere, that rainbow work of fancy that clothes what is naked and seems to ennoble what is base;

in each, life falls dead like dough, instead of soaring away like a balloon into the colours of the sunset; each is true, each inconceivable; for no man lives in the external truth, among salts and acids, but in the warm, phantasmagoric chamber of his brain, with the painted windows and the storied walls.

Of this falsity we have had a recent example from a man who knows far better—Tolstoi's *Powers of Darkness*. Here is a piece full of force and truth, yet quite untrue. For before Mikita was led into so dire a situation he was tempted, and temptations are beautiful at least in part; and a work which dwells on the ugliness of crime and gives no hint of any loveliness in the temptation, sins against the modesty of life, and even when a Tolstoi writes it, sinks to melodrama. The peasants are not understood; they saw their life in fairer colours; even the deaf girl was clothed in poetry for Mikita, or he had never fallen. And so, once again, even an Old Bailey melodrama, without some brightness of poetry and lustre of existence, falls into the inconceivable and ranks with fairy tales.

IV

In nobler books we are moved with something like the emotions of life; and this emotion is very variously provoked. We are so moved when Levine labours in the field, when André sinks beyond emotion, when Richard Feverel and Lucy Desborough meet beside the river, when Antony, 'not cowardly, puts off his helmet,' when Kent has infinite pity on the dying Lear, when, in Dostoieffky's *Despised and Rejected*, the uncomplaining hero drains his cup of suffering and virtue. These are notes that please the great heart of man. Not only love, and the fields, and the bright face of danger, but sacrifice and death and unmerited suffering humbly supported, touch in us the vein of the poetic. We love to think of them, we long to try them, we are humbly hopeful that we may prove heroes also.

We have heard, perhaps, too much of lesser matters. Here is the door, here is the open air. *Itur in antiquam silvam.*

VIII

A CHAPTER ON DREAMS

THE past is all of one texture — whether
feigned or suffered — whether acted out in
three dimensions, or only witnessed in that
small theatre of the brain which we keep
brightly lighted all night long, after the jets
are down, and darkness and sleep reign
undisturbed in the remainder of the body.
There is no distinction on the face of our
experiences; one is vivid indeed, and one dull,
and one pleasant, and another agonising to
remember; but which of them is what we call
true, and which a dream, there is not one hair
to prove. The past stands on a precarious
footing; another straw split in the field of
metaphysic, and behold us robbed of it.
There is scarce a family that can count four
generations but lays a claim to some dormant

title or some castle and estate: a claim not
prosecutable in any court of law, but flattering
to the fancy and a great alleviation of idle
hours. A man's claim to his own past is yet
less valid. A paper might turn up (in proper
story-book fashion) in the secret drawer of an
old ebony secretary, and restore your family
to its ancient honours, and reinstate mine in a
certain West Indian islet (not far from St.
Kitt's, as beloved tradition hummed in my
young ears) which was once ours, and is now
unjustly someone else's, and for that matter
(in the state of the sugar trade) is not worth
anything to anybody. I do not say that these
revolutions are likely; only no man can deny
that they are possible; and the past, on the
other hand, is lost for ever: our old days and
deeds, our old selves, too, and the very world
in which these scenes were acted, all brought
down to the same faint residuum as a last
night's dream, to some incontinuous images,
and an echo in the chambers of the brain.
Not an hour, not a mood, not a glance of
the eye, can we revoke; it is all gone, past
conjuring. And yet conceive us robbed of it,

conceive that little thread of memory that we
trail behind us broken at the pocket's edge;
and in what naked nullity should we be left!
for we only guide ourselves, and only know ourselves, by these air-painted pictures of the past.

Upon these grounds, there are some among
us who claimed to have lived longer and more
richly than their neighbours; when they lay
asleep they claim they were still active; and
among the treasures of memory that all men
review for their amusement, these count in no
second place the harvests of their dreams.
There is one of this kind whom I have in my
eye, and whose case is perhaps unusual enough
to be described. He was from a child an
ardent and uncomfortable dreamer. When he
had a touch of fever at night, and the room
swelled and shrank, and his clothes, hanging
on a nail, now loomed up instant to the big-
ness of a church, and now drew away into a
horror of infinite distance and infinite littleness,
the poor soul was very well aware of what
must follow, and struggled hard against the
approaches of that slumber which was the
beginning of sorrows. But his struggles were

in vain; sooner or later the night-hag would have him by the throat, and pluck him, strangling and screaming, from his sleep. His dreams were at times commonplace enough, at times very strange : at times they were almost formless, he would be haunted, for instance, by nothing more definite than a certain hue of brown, which he did not mind in the least while he was awake, but feared and loathed while he was dreaming; at times, again, they took on every detail of circumstance, as when once he supposed he must swallow the populous world, and awoke screaming with the horror of the thought. The two chief troubles of his very narrow existence—the practical and everyday trouble of school tasks and the ultimate and airy one of hell and judgment—were often confounded together into one appalling nightmare. He seemed to himself to stand before the Great White Throne; he was called on, poor little devil, to recite some form of words, on which his destiny depended; his tongue stuck, his memory was blank, hell gaped for him; and he would awake, clinging to the curtain-rod with his knees to his chin.

These were extremely poor experiences, on the whole; and at that time of life my dreamer would have very willingly parted with his power of dreams. But presently, in the course of his growth, the cries and physical contortions passed away, seemingly for ever; his visions were still for the most part miserable, but they were more constantly supported; and he would awake with no more extreme symptom than a flying heart, a freezing scalp, cold sweats, and the speechless midnight fear. His dreams, too, as befitted a mind better stocked with particulars, became more circumstantial, and had more the air and continuity of life. The look of the world beginning to take hold on his attention, scenery came to play a part in his sleeping as well as in his waking thoughts, so that he would take long, uneventful journeys and see strange towns and beautiful places as he lay in bed. And, what is more significant, an odd taste that he had for the Georgian costume and for stories laid in that period of English history, began to rule the features of his dreams; so that he masqueraded there in a three-cornered hat, and

was much engaged with Jacobite conspiracy
between the hour for bed and that for breakfast. About the same time, he began to read
in his dreams—tales, for the most part, and
for the most part after the manner of G. P.
R. James, but so incredibly more vivid and
moving than any printed book, that he has
ever since been malcontent with literature.

And then, while he was yet a student, there
came to him a dream-adventure which he has no
anxiety to repeat; he began, that is to say, to
dream in sequence and thus to lead a double
life—one of the day, one of the night—one
that he had every reason to believe was the
true one, another that he had no means of
proving to be false. I should have said he
studied, or was by way of studying, at Edin-
burgh College, which (it may be supposed) was
how I came to know him. Well, in his dream-
life, he passed a long day in the surgical theatre,
his heart in his mouth, his teeth on edge, seeing
monstrous malformations and the abhorred
dexterity of surgeons. In a heavy, rainy,
foggy evening he came forth into the South
Bridge, turned up the High Street, and entered

the door of a tall *land*, at the top of which he
supposed himself to lodge. All night long, in
his wet clothes, he climbed the stairs, stair after
stair in endless series, and at every second flight
a flaring lamp with a reflector. All night long,
he brushed by single persons passing downward
—beggarly women of the street, great, weary,
muddy labourers, poor scarecrows of men, pale
parodies of women—but all drowsy and weary
like himself, and all single, and all brushing
against him as they passed. In the end, out of
a northern window, he would see day beginning
to whiten over the Firth, give up the ascent,
turn to descend, and in a breath be back again
upon the streets, in his wet clothes, in the wet,
haggard dawn, trudging to another day of mon-
strosities and operations. Time went quicker
in the life of dreams, some seven hours (as near
as he can guess) to one; and it went, besides,
more intensely, so that the gloom of these fan-
cied experiences clouded the day, and he had
not shaken off their shadow ere it was time to
lie down and to renew them. I cannot tell how
long it was that he endured this discipline; but
it was long enough to leave a great black blot

upon his memory, long enough to send him, trembling for his reason, to the doors of a certain doctor; whereupon with a simple draught he was restored to the common lot of man.

The poor gentleman has since been troubled by nothing of the sort; indeed, his nights were for some while like other men's, now blank, now chequered with dreams, and these sometimes charming, sometimes appalling, but except for an occasional vividness, of no extraordinary kind. I will just note one of these occasions, ere I pass on to what makes my dreamer truly interesting. It seemed to him that he was in the first floor of a rough hill-farm. The room showed some poor efforts at gentility, a carpet on the floor, a piano, I think, against the wall; but, for all these refinements, there was no mistaking he was in a moorland place, among hillside people, and set in miles of heather. He looked down from the window upon a bare farmyard, that seemed to have been long disused. A great, uneasy stillness lay upon the world. There was no sign of the farm-folk or of any live stock, save for an old, brown, curly dog of the retriever breed, who sat close in against the wall of the house and seemed to be dozing. Something about this dog disquieted the dreamer; it was quite a nameless feeling, for the beast looked right enough—indeed, he was so old and dull and dusty and broken-down, that he should rather have awakened pity; and yet the conviction came and grew upon the dreamer that this was no proper dog at all, but something hellish. A great many dozing summer flies hummed about the yard; and presently the dog thrust forth his paw, caught a fly in his open palm, carried it to his mouth like an ape, and looking suddenly up at the dreamer in the window, winked to him with one eye. The dream went on, it matters not how it went; it was a good dream as dreams go; but there was nothing in the sequel worthy of that devilish brown dog. And the point of interest for me lies partly in that very fact: that having found so singular an incident, my imperfect dreamer should prove unable to carry the tale to a fit end and fall back on indescribable noises and indiscriminate horrors. It would be different now; he knows his business better!

For, to approach at last the point: This honest fellow had long been in the custom of setting himself to sleep with tales, and so had his father before him; but these were irresponsible inventions, told for the teller's pleasure, with no eye to the crass public or the thwart reviewer: tales where a thread might be dropped, or one adventure quitted for another, on fancy's least suggestion. So that the little people who manage man's internal theatre had not as yet received a very rigorous training; and played upon their stage like children who should have slipped into the house and found it empty, rather than like drilled actors performing a set piece to a huge hall of faces. But presently my dreamer began to turn his former amusement of story-telling to (what is called) account; by which I mean that he began to write and sell his tales. Here was he, and here were the little people who did that part of his business, in quite new conditions. The stories must now be trimmed and pared and set upon all fours, they must run from a beginning to an end and fit (after a manner) with the laws of life; the pleasure, in one word,

had become a business ; and that not only for the
dreamer, but for the little people of his theatre.
These understood the change as well as he.
When he lay down to prepare himself for sleep,
he no longer sought amusement, but printable
and profitable tales ; and after he had dozed
off in his box-seat, his little people continued
their evolutions with the same mercantile de-
signs. All other forms of dream deserted him
but two: he still occasionally reads the most
delightful books, he still visits at times the most
delightful places; and it is perhaps worthy
of note that to these same places, and to one
in particular, he returns at intervals of months
and years, finding new field-paths, visiting new
neighbours, beholding that happy valley under
new effects of noon and dawn and sunset. But
all the rest of the family of visions is quite lost
to him: the common, mangled version of yesterday's affairs, the raw-head-and-bloody-bones
nightmare, rumoured to be the child of toasted
cheese—these and their like are gone ; and, for
the most part, whether awake or asleep, he is
simply occupied—he or his little people—in
consciously making stories for the market.

This dreamer (like many other persons) has encountered some trifling vicissitudes of fortune. When the bank begins to send letters and the butcher to linger at the back gate, he sets to belabouring his brains after a story, for that is his readiest money-winner; and, behold! at once the little people begin to bestir themselves in the same quest, and labour all night long, and all night long set before him truncheons of tales upon their lighted theatre. No fear of his being frightened now; the flying heart and the frozen scalp are things bygone; applause, growing applause, growing interest, growing exultation in his own cleverness (for he takes all the credit), and at last a jubilant leap to wakefulness, with the cry, 'I have it, that'll do!' upon his lips: with such and similar emotions he sits at these nocturnal dramas, with such outbreaks, like Claudius in the play, he scatters the performance in the midst. Often enough the waking is a disappointment: he has been too deep asleep, as I explain the thing; drowsiness has gained his little people, they have gone stumbling and maundering through their parts; and the play, to the awakened mind, is seen to be a tissue of absurdities. And yet how often have these sleepless Brownies done him honest service, and given him, as he sat idly taking his pleasure in the boxes, better tales than he could fashion for himself.

Here is one, exactly as it came to him. It seemed he was the son of a very rich and wicked man, the owner of broad acres and a most damnable temper. The dreamer (and that was the son) had lived much abroad, on purpose to avoid his parent; and when at length he returned to England, it was to find him married again to a young wife, who was supposed to suffer cruelly and to loathe her yoke. Because of this marriage (as the dreamer indistinctly understood) it was desirable for father and son to have a meeting; and yet both being proud and both angry, neither would condescend upon a visit. Meet they did accordingly, in a desolate, sandy country by the sea; and there they quarrelled, and the son, stung by some intolerable insult, struck down the father dead. No suspicion was aroused; the dead man was found and buried, and the dreamer succeeded to the broad estates, and found himself installed under the same roof with his father's widow, for whom no provision had been made. These two lived very much alone, as people may after a bereavement, sat down to table together, shared the long evenings, and grew daily better friends; until it seemed to him of a sudden that she was prying about dangerous matters, that she had conceived a notion of his guilt, that she watched him and tried him with questions. He drew back from her company as men draw back from a precipice suddenly discovered; and yet so strong was the attraction that he would drift again and again into the old intimacy, and again and again be startled back by some suggestive question or some inexplicable meaning in her eye. So they lived at cross purposes, a life full of broken dialogue, challenging glances, and suppressed passion; until, one day, he saw the woman slipping from the house in a veil, followed her to the station, followed her in the train to the seaside country, and out over the sandhills to the very place where the murder was done. There she began to grope among the bents, he watching her, flat upon his face; and presently she had something in her hand— I cannot remember what it was, but it was deadly evidence against the dreamer—and as she held it up to look at it, perhaps from the shock of the discovery, her foot slipped, and she hung at some peril on the brink of the tall sand-wreaths. He had no thought but to spring up and rescue her; and there they stood face to face, she with that deadly matter openly in her hand—his very presence on the spot another link of proof. It was plain she was about to speak, but this was more than he could bear—he could bear to be lost, but not to talk of it with his destroyer; and he cut her short with trivial conversation. Arm in arm, they returned together to the train, talking he knew not what, made the journey back in the same carriage, sat down to dinner, and passed the evening in the drawing-room as in the past. But suspense and fear drummed in the dreamer's bosom. 'She has not denounced me yet'—so his thoughts ran—'when will she denounce me? Will it be to-morrow?' And it was not to-morrow, nor the next day, nor the next; and

their life settled back on the old terms, only
that she seemed kinder than before, and that,
as for him, the burthen of his suspense and
wonder grew daily more unbearable, so that he
wasted away like a man with a disease. Once,
indeed, he broke all bounds of decency, seized
an occasion when she was abroad, ransacked
her room, and at last, hidden away among her
jewels, found the damning evidence. There he
stood, holding this thing, which was his life, in
the hollow of his hand, and marvelling at her
inconsequent behaviour, that she should seek,
and keep, and yet not use it; and then the
door opened, and behold herself. So, once
more, they stood, eye to eye, with the evidence
between them; and once more she raised to
him a face brimming with some communication;
and once more he shied away from speech and
cut her off. But before he left the room, which
he had turned upside down, he laid back his
death-warrant where he had found it; and at
that, her face lighted up. The next thing he
heard, she was explaining to her maid, with
some ingenious falsehood, the disorder of her
things. Flesh and blood could bear the strain

no longer; and I think it was the next morning (though chronology is always hazy in the theatre of the mind) that he burst from his reserve. They had been breakfasting together in one corner of a great, parqueted, sparely-furnished room of many windows; all the time of the meal she had tortured him with sly allusions; and no sooner were the servants gone, and these two protagonists alone together, than he leaped to his feet. She too sprang up, with a pale face; with a pale face, she heard him as he raved out his complaint: Why did she torture him so? she knew all, she knew he was no enemy to her; why did she not denounce him at once? what signified her whole behaviour? why did she torture him? and yet again, why did she torture him? And when he had done, she fell upon her knees, and with outstretched hands: 'Do you not understand?' she cried. 'I love you!'

Hereupon, with a pang of wonder and mercantile delight, the dreamer awoke. His mercantile delight was not of long endurance; for it soon became plain that in this spirited tale there were unmarketable elements; which

is just the reason why you have it here so
briefly told. But his wonder has still kept
growing; and I think the reader's will also, if
he consider it ripely. For now he sees why I
speak of the little people as of substantive
inventors and performers. To the end they
had kept their secret. I will go bail for the
dreamer (having excellent grounds for valuing
his candour) that he had no guess whatever at
the motive of the woman—the hinge of the
whole well-invented plot—until the instant of
that highly dramatic declaration. It was not
his tale; it was the little people's! And
observe : not only was the secret kept, the
story was told with really guileful craftsman-
ship. The conduct of both actors is (in the
cant phrase) psychologically correct, and the
emotion aptly graduated up to the surprising
climax. I am awake now, and I know this
trade; and yet I cannot better it. I am awake,
and I live by this business; and yet I could
not outdo — could not perhaps equal — that
crafty artifice (as of some old, experienced carpenter of plays, some Dennery or Sardou) by
which the same situation is twice presented and

the two actors twice brought face to face over the evidence, only once it is in her hand, once in his—and these in their due order, the least dramatic first. The more I think of it, the more I am moved to press upon the world my question : Who are the Little People ? They are near connections of the dreamer's, beyond doubt; they share in his financial worries and have an eye to the bank-book; they share plainly in his training; they have plainly learned like him to build the scheme of a considerate story and to arrange emotion in progressive order; only I think they have more talent; and one thing is beyond doubt, they can tell him a story piece by piece, like a serial, and keep him all the while in ignorance of where they aim. Who are they, then ? and who is the dreamer ?

Well, as regards the dreamer, I can answer that, for he is no less a person than myself ;— as I might have told you from the beginning, only that the critics murmur over my consistent egotism ;—and as I am positively forced to tell you now, or I could advance but little farther with my story. And for the Little People,

what shall I say they are but just my Brownies,
God bless them! who do one-half my work for
me while I am fast asleep, and in all human
likelihood, do the rest for me as well, when I
am wide awake and fondly suppose I do it for
myself. That part which is done while I am
sleeping is the Brownies' part beyond contention; but that which is done when I am up and
about is by no means necessarily mine, since all
goes to show the Brownies have a hand in it
even then. Here is a doubt that much concerns
my conscience. For myself—what I call I, my
conscious ego, the denizen of the pineal gland
unless he has changed his residence since Des-
cartes, the man with the conscience and the
variable bank-account, the man with the hat
and the boots, and the privilege of voting and
not carrying his candidate at the general elec-
tions—I am sometimes tempted to suppose he
is no story-teller at all, but a creature as matter
of fact as any cheesemonger or any cheese, and
a realist bemired up to the ears in actuality; so
that, by that account, the whole of my published
fiction should be the single-handed product of
some Brownie, some Familiar, some unseen

collaborator, whom I keep locked in a back garret, while I get all the praise and he but a share (which I cannot prevent him getting) of the pudding. I am an excellent adviser, something like Molière's servant; I pull back and I cut down; and I dress the whole in the best words and sentences that I can find and make; I hold the pen, too; and I do the sitting at the table, which is about the worst of it; and when all is done, I make up the manuscript and pay for the registration; so that, on the whole, I have some claim to share, though not so largely as I do, in the profits of our common enterprise.

I can but give an instance or so of what part is done sleeping and what part awake, and leave the reader to share what laurels there are, at his own nod, between myself and my collaborators; and to do this I will first take a book that a number of persons have been polite enough to read, the *Strange Case of Dr. Jekyll and Mr. Hyde.* I had long been trying to write a story on this subject, to find a body, a vehicle, for that strong sense of man's double being which must at times come in upon and overwhelm the mind of every thinking creature.

I had even written one, *The Travelling Companion*, which was returned by an editor on the plea that it was a work of genius and indecent, and which I burned the other day on the ground that it was not a work of genius, and that *Jekyll* had supplanted it. Then came one of those financial fluctuations to which (with an elegant modesty) I have hitherto referred in the third person. For two days I went about racking my brains for a plot of any sort; and on the second night I dreamed the scene at the window, and a scene afterwards split in two, in which Hyde, pursued for some crime, took the powder and underwent the change in the presence of his pursuers. All the rest was made awake, and consciously, although I think I can trace in much of it the manner of my Brownies. The meaning of the tale is therefore mine, and had long pre-existed in my garden of Adonis, and tried one body after another in vain; indeed, I do most of the morality, worse luck! and my Brownies have not a rudiment of what we call a conscience. Mine, too, is the setting, mine the characters. All that was given me was the matter of three scenes, and

the central idea of a voluntary change becoming involuntary. Will it be thought ungenerous,
after I have been so liberally ladling out praise
to my unseen collaborators, if I here toss them
over, bound hand and foot, into the arena of
the critics? For the business of the powders,
which so many have censured, is, I am relieved
to say, not mine at all but the Brownies'. Of
another tale, in case the reader should have
glanced at it, I may say a word : the not very
defensible story of *Olalla.* Here the court, the
mother, the mother's niche, Olalla, Olalla's
chamber, the meetings on the stair, the broken
window, the ugly scene of the bite, were all
given me in bulk and detail as I have tried to
write them ; to this I added only the external
scenery (for in my dream I never was beyond
the court), the portrait, the characters of Felipe
and the priest, the moral, such as it is, and the
last pages, such as, alas! they are. And I may
even say that in this case the moral itself was
given me ; for it arose immediately on a comparison of the mother and the daughter, and
from the hideous trick of atavism in the first.
Sometimes a parabolic sense is still more unde-

niably present in a dream; sometimes I cannot
but suppose my Brownies have been aping
Bunyan, and yet in no case with what would
possibly be called a moral in a tract; never
with the ethical narrowness; conveying hints
instead of life's larger limitations and that sort
of sense which we seem to perceive in the arabesque of time and space.

For the most part, it will be seen, my Brownies
are somewhat fantastic, like their stories hot and
hot, full of passion and the picturesque, alive
with animating incident; and they have no prejudice against the supernatural.   But the other
day they gave me a surprise, entertaining me
with a love-story, a little April comedy, which I
ought certainly to hand over to the author of
A Chance Acquaintance, for he could write it as
it should be written, and I am sure (although I
mean to try) that I cannot.—But who would
have supposed that a Brownie of mine should
invent a tale for Mr. Howells?

IX

BEGGARS

I

In a pleasant, airy, up-hill country, it was my
fortune when I was young to make the acquaintance of a certain beggar. I call him beggar,
though he usually allowed his coat and his
shoes (which were open-mouthed, indeed) to
beg for him. He was the wreck of an athletic
man, tall, gaunt, and bronzed; far gone in con-
sumption, with that disquieting smile of the
mortally stricken on his face; but still active
afoot, still with the brisk military carriage, the
ready military salute. Three ways led through
this piece of country; and as I was inconstant
in my choice, I believe he must often have
awaited me in vain. But often enough, he
caught me; often enough, from some place of

ambush by the roadside, he would spring suddenly forth in the regulation attitude, and launching at once into his inconsequential talk, fall into step with me upon my farther course. ' A fine morning, sir, though perhaps a trifle inclining to rain. I hope I see you well, sir. Why, no, sir, I don't feel as hearty myself as I could wish, but I am keeping about my ordinary. I am pleased to meet you on the road, sir. I assure you I quite look forward to one of our little conversations.' He loved the sound of his own voice inordinately, and though (with something too off-hand to call servility) he would always hasten to agree with anything you said, yet he could never suffer you to say it to an end. By what transition he slid to his favourite subject I have no memory; but we had never been long together on the way before he was dealing, in a very military manner, with the English poets. ' Shelley was a fine poet, sir, though a trifle atheistical in his opinions. His Queen Mab, sir, is quite an atheistical work. Scott, sir, is not so poetical a writer. With the works of Shakespeare I am not so well acquainted, but he was a fine poet. Keats—John Keats, sir—he was a very fine poet.' With such references, such trivial criticism, such loving parade of his own knowledge, he would beguile the road, striding forward up-hill, his staff now clapped to the ribs of his deep, resonant chest, now swinging in the air with the remembered jauntiness of the private soldier; and all the while his toes looking out of his boots, and his shirt looking out of his elbows, and death looking out of his smile, and his big, crazy frame shaken by accesses of cough.

He would often go the whole way home with me: often to borrow a book, and that book always a poet. Off he would march, to continue his mendicant rounds, with the volume slipped into the pocket of his ragged coat; and although he would sometimes keep it quite a while, yet it came always back again at last, not much the worse for its travels into beggardom. And in this way, doubtless, his knowledge grew and his glib, random criticism took a wider range. But my library was not the first he had drawn upon:

at our first encounter, he was already brimful
of Shelley and the atheistical Queen Mab, and
'Keats—John Keats, sir.' And I have often
wondered how he came by these acquirements;
just as I often wondered how he fell to be a
beggar. He had served through the Mutiny—
of which (like so many people) he could tell
practically nothing beyond the names of places,
and that it was 'difficult work, sir,' and very
hot, or that so-and-so was 'a very fine com-
mander, sir.' He was far too smart a man to
have remained a private; in the nature of
things, he must have won his stripes. And
yet here he was without a pension. When I
touched on this problem, he would content
himself with diffidently offering me advice.
'A man should be very careful when he is
young, sir. If you'll excuse me saying so, a
spirited young gentleman like yourself, sir,
should be very careful. I was perhaps a trifle
inclined to atheistical opinions myself.' For
(perhaps with a deeper wisdom than we are
inclined in these days to admit) he plainly
bracketed agnosticism with beer and skittles.

Keats—John Keats, sir—and Shelley were

his favourite bards.   I cannot remember if I
tried him with Rossetti ; but I know his taste
to a hair, and if ever I did, he must have doted
on that author.   What took him was a richness
in the speech ; he loved the exotic, the unex-
pected word ; the moving cadence of a phrase ;
a vague sense of emotion (about nothing) in
the very letters of the alphabet : the romance
of language.   His honest head was very nearly
empty, his intellect like a child's ; and when he
read his favourite authors, he can almost never
have understood what he was reading.   Yet the
taste was not only genuine, it was exclusive ; I
tried in vain to offer him novels ; he would
none of them, he cared for nothing but romantic
language that he could not understand.   The
case may be commoner than we suppose.   I
am reminded of a lad who was laid in the next
cot to a friend of mine in a public hospital,
and who was no sooner installed than he sent
out (perhaps with his last pence) for a cheap
Shakespeare.   My friend pricked up his ears ;
fell at once in talk with his new neighbour, and
was ready, when the book arrived, to make a
singular discovery.   For this lover of great

literature understood not one sentence out of twelve, and his favourite part was that of which he understood the least—the inimitable, mouth-filling rodomontade of the ghost in *Hamlet*. It was a bright day in hospital when my friend expounded the sense of this beloved jargon: a task for which I am willing to believe my friend was very fit, though I can never regard it as an easy one. I know indeed a point or two, on which I would gladly question Mr. Shakespeare, that lover of big words, could he revisit the glimpses of the moon, or could I myself climb backward to the spacious days of Elizabeth. But in the second case, I should most likely pretermit these questionings, and take my place instead in the pit at the Black-friars, to hear the actor in his favourite part, playing up to Mr. Burbage, and rolling out—as I seem to hear him—with a ponderous gusto—

'Unhousel'd, disappointed, unanel'd.'

What a pleasant chance, if we could go there in a party! and what a surprise for Mr. Bur-bage, when the ghost received the honours of the evening!

As for my old soldier, like Mr. Burbage and Mr. Shakespeare, he is long since dead; and now lies buried, I suppose, and nameless and quite forgotten, in some poor city graveyard.— But not for me, you brave heart, have you been buried! For me, you are still afoot, tasting the sun and air, and striding southward. By the groves of Comiston and beside the Hermitage of Braid, by the Hunters' Tryst, and where the curlews and plovers cry around Fairmilehead, I see and hear you, stalwartly carrying your deadly sickness, cheerfully discoursing of un-comprehended poets.

II

The thought of the old soldier recalls that of another tramp, his counterpart. This was a little, lean, and fiery man, with the eyes of a dog and the face of a gipsy; whom I found one morning encamped with his wife and children and his grinder's wheel, beside the burn of Kinnaird. To this beloved dell I went, at that time, daily; and daily the knife-grinder and I (for as long as his tent continued pleasantly to interrupt my little wilderness) sat on two stones, and smoked, and plucked grass, and talked to the tune of the brown water. His children were mere whelps, they fought and bit among the fern like vermin. His wife was a mere squaw; I saw her gather brush and tend the kettle, but she never ventured to address her lord while I was present. The tent was a mere gipsy hovel, like a sty for pigs. But the grinder himself had the fine self-sufficiency and grave politeness of the hunter and the savage; he did me the honours of this dell, which had been mine but the day before, took me far into the secrets of his life, and used me (I am proud to remember) as a friend.

Like my old soldier, he was far gone in the national complaint. Unlike him, he had a vulgar taste in letters; scarce flying higher than the story papers; probably finding no difference, certainly seeking none, between Tannahill and Burns; his noblest thoughts, whether of poetry or music, adequately embodied in that somewhat obvious ditty,

> 'Will ye gang, lassie, gang
> To the braes o' Balquidder:'

—which is indeed apt to echo in the ears of

Scottish children, and to him, in view of his
experience, must have found a special directness
of address. But if he had no fine sense of
poetry in letters, he felt with a deep joy the
poetry of life. You should have heard him
speak of what he loved; of the tent pitched
beside the talking water; of the stars overhead
at night; of the blest return of morning, the
peep of day over the moors, the awaking birds
among the birches ; how he abhorred the long
winter shut in cities ; and with what delight, at
the return of the spring, he once more pitched
his camp in the living out-of-doors. But we
were a pair of tramps; and to you, who are
doubtless sedentary and a consistent first-class
passenger in life, he would scarce have laid
himself so open ;—to you, he might have been
content to tell his story of a ghost—that of a
buccaneer with his pistols as he lived—whom
he had once encountered in a seaside cave
near Buckie; and that would have been enough,
for that would have shown you the mettle of
the man. Here was a piece of experience solidly
and livingly built up in words, here was a story
created, *teres atque rotundus*

And to think of the old soldier, that lover of the literary bards! He had visited stranger spots than any seaside cave; encountered men more terrible than any spirit; done and dared and suffered in that incredible, unsung epic of the Mutiny War; played his part with the field force of Delhi, beleaguering and beleaguered; shared in that enduring, savage anger and contempt of death and decency that, for long months together, bedevil'd and inspired the army; was hurled to and fro in the battle-smoke of the assault; was there, perhaps, where Nicholson fell; was there when the attacking column, with hell upon every side, found the soldier's enemy—strong drink, and the lives of tens of thousands trembled in the scale, and the fate of the flag of England staggered. And of all this he had no more to say than 'hot work, sir,' or 'the army suffered a great deal, sir,' or 'I believe General Wilson, sir, was not very highly thought of in the papers.' His life was naught to him, the vivid pages of experience quite blank: in words his pleasure lay— melodious, agitated words — printed words, about that which he had never seen and was

connatally incapable of comprehending. We
have here two temperaments face to face; both
untrained, unsophisticated, surprised (we may
say) in the egg; both boldly charactered :—
that of the artist, the lover and artificer of
words; that of the maker, the seeër, the lover
and forger of experience. If the one had a
daughter and the other had a son, and these
married, might not some illustrious writer count
descent from the beggar-soldier and the needy
knife-grinder?

III

Every one lives by selling something, whatever be his right to it. The burglar sells at
the same time his own skill and courage and
my silver plate (the whole at the most moderate
figure) to a Jew receiver. The bandit sells
the traveller an article of prime necessity : that
traveller's life. And as for the old soldier, who
stands for central mark to my capricious figures
of eight, he dealt in a specialty; for he was
the only beggar in the world who ever gave me
pleasure for my money. He had learned a

school of manners in the barracks and had the sense to cling to it, accosting strangers with a regimental freedom, thanking patrons with a merely regimental difference, sparing you at once the tragedy of his position and the embarrassment of yours. There was not one hint about him of the beggar's emphasis, the outburst of revolting gratitude, the rant and cant, the 'God bless you, Kind, Kind gentleman,' which insults the smallness of your alms by disproportionate vehemence, which is so notably false, which would be so unbearable if it were true. I am sometimes tempted to suppose this reading of the beggar's part, a survival of the old days when Shakespeare was intoned upon the stage and mourners keened beside the death-bed; to think that we cannot now accept these strong emotions unless they be uttered in the just note of life; nor (save in the pulpit) endure these gross conventions. They wound us, I am tempted to say, like mockery; the high voice of keening (as it yet lingers on) strikes in the face of sorrow like a buffet; and the rant and cant of the staled beggar stirs in us a shudder of disgust. But the fact disproves these amateur opinions. The beggar lives by his knowledge of the average man. He knows what he is about when he bandages his head, and hires and drugs a babe, and poisons life with *Poor Mary Ann* or *Long, long ago;* he knows what he is about when he loads the critical ear and sickens the nice conscience with intolerable thanks; they know what they are about, he and his crew, when they pervade the slums of cities, ghastly parodies of suffering, hateful parodies of gratitude. This trade can scarce be called an imposition; it has been so blown upon with exposures; it flaunts its fraudulence so nakedly. We pay them as we pay those who show us, in huge exaggeration, the monsters of our drinking-water; or those who daily predict the fall of Britain. We pay them for the pain they inflict, pay them, and wince, and hurry on. And truly there is nothing that can shake the conscience like a beggar's thanks; and that polity in which such protestations can be purchased for a shilling, seems no scene for an honest man.

Are there, then, we may be asked, no genuine

beggars? And the answer is, Not one. My old soldier was a humbug like the rest; his ragged boots were, in the stage phrase, properties; whole boots were given him again and again, and always gladly accepted; and the next day, there he was on the road as usual, with toes exposed. His boots were his method; they were the man's trade; without his boots he would have starved; he did not live by charity, but by appealing to a gross taste in the public, which loves the limelight on the actor's face, and the toes out of the beggar's boots. There is a true poverty, which no one sees: a false and merely mimetic poverty, which usurps its place and dress, and lives and above all drinks, on the fruits of the usurpation. The true poverty does not go into the streets; the banker may rest assured, he has never put a penny in its hand. The self-respecting poor beg from each other; never from the rich. To live in the frock-coated ranks of life, to hear canting scenes of gratitude rehearsed for twopence, a man might suppose that giving was a thing gone out of fashion; yet it goes forward on a scale so great as to fill me with surprise. In the houses of the working class, all day long there will be a foot upon the stair; all day long there will be a knocking at the doors; beggars come, beggars go, without stint, hardly with intermission, from morning till night; and meanwhile, in the same city and but a few streets off, the castles of the rich stand unsummoned. Get the tale of any honest tramp, you will find it was always the poor who helped him; get the truth from any workman who has met misfortunes, it was always next door that he would go for help, or only with such exceptions as are said to prove a rule; look at the course of the mimetic beggar, it is through the poor quarters that he trails his passage, showing his bandages to every window, piercing even to the attics with his nasal song. Here is a remarkable state of things in our Christian commonwealths, that the poor only should be asked to give.

IV

There is a pleasant tale of some worthless, phrasing Frenchman, who was taxed with ingratitude : '*Il faut savoir garder l'indé-pendance du cœur,*' cried he.   I own I feel with him.   Gratitude without familiarity, gratitude otherwise than as a nameless element in a friendship, is a thing so near to hatred that I do not care to split the difference.   Until I find a man who is pleased to receive obliga-tions, I shall continue to question the tact of those who are eager to confer them.   What an art it is, to give, even to our nearest friends ! and what a test of manners, to receive !   How, upon either side, we smuggle away the obli-gation, blushing for each other ; how bluff and dull we make the giver ; how hasty, how falsely cheerful, the receiver !   And yet an act of such difficulty and distress between near friends, it is supposed we can perform to a total stranger and leave the man transfixed with grateful emotions.   The last thing you can do to a man is to burthen him with an obligation, and it is what we propose to begin with! But let us not be deceived: unless he is totally degraded to his trade, anger jars in his inside, and he grates his teeth at our gratuity.

We should wipe two words from our vocabulary: gratitude and charity. In real life, help is given out of friendship, or it is not valued; it is received from the hand of friendship, or it is resented. We are all too proud to take a naked gift: we must seem to pay it, if in nothing else, then with the delights of our society. Here, then, is the pitiful fix of the rich man; here is that needle's eye in which he stuck already in the days of Christ, and still sticks to-day, firmer, if possible, than ever: that he has the money and lacks the love which should make his money acceptable. Here and now, just as of old in Palestine, he has the rich to dinner, it is with the rich that he takes his pleasure: and when his turn comes to be charitable, he looks in vain for a recipient. His friends are not poor, they do not want; the poor are not his friends, they will not take. To whom is he to give? Where to find—note this phrase—the Deserv-

ing Poor? Charity is (what they call) central-
ised; offices are hired; societies founded,
with secretaries paid or unpaid: the hunt of
the Deserving Poor goes merrily forward.
I think it will take more than a merely human
secretary to disinter that character. What!
a class that is to be in want from no fault
of its own, and yet greedily eager to receive
from strangers; and to be quite respectable,
and at the same time quite devoid of self-
respect; and play the most delicate part of
friendship, and yet never be seen; and wear
the form of man, and yet fly in the face of all
the laws of human nature:—and all this, in the
hope of getting a belly-god Burgess through
a needle's eye! O, let him stick, by all means:
and let his polity tumble in the dust; and
let his epitaph and all his literature (of which
my own works begin to form no inconsiderable
part) be abolished even from the history of
man! For a fool of this monstrosity of dulness, there can be no salvation: and the fool
who looked for the elixir of life was an angel
of reason to the fool who looks for the Deserving Poor!

V

And yet there is one course which the unfortunate gentleman may take. He may subscribe to pay the taxes. There were the true charity, impartial and impersonal, cumbering none with obligation, helping all. There were a destination for loveless gifts; there were the way to reach the pocket of the deserving poor, and yet save the time of secretaries! But, alas! there is no colour of romance in such a course; and people nowhere demand the picturesque so much as in their virtues.

X

LETTER TO A YOUNG GENTLEMAN WHO PROPOSES TO EMBRACE THE CAREER OF ART

With the agreeable frankness of youth, you address me on a point of some practical importance to yourself and (it is even conceivable) of some gravity to the world : Should you or should you not become an artist? It is one which you must decide entirely for yourself; all that I can do is to bring under your notice some of the materials of that decision; and I will begin, as I shall probably conclude also, by assuring you that all depends on the vocation.

To know what you like is the beginning of wisdom and of old age. Youth is wholly experimental. The essence and charm of that

272

unquiet and delightful epoch is ignorance of self as well as ignorance of life. These two unknowns the young man brings together again and again, now in the airiest touch, now with a bitter hug; now with exquisite pleasure, now with cutting pain; but never with indifference, to which he is a total stranger, and never with that near kinsman of indifference, contentment. If he be a youth of dainty senses or a brain easily heated, the interest of this series of experiments grows upon him out of all proportion to the pleasure he receives. It is not beauty that he loves, nor pleasure that he seeks, though he may think so; his design and his sufficient reward is to verify his own existence and taste the variety of human fate. To him, before the razor-edge of curiosity is dulled, all that is not actual living and the hot chase of experience wears a face of a disgusting dryness difficult to recall in later days; or if there be any exception—and here destiny steps in—it is in those moments when, wearied or surfeited of the primary activity of the senses, he calls up before memory the image of transacted pains and pleasures. Thus it is that such an one shies from all cut-and-dry professions, and inclines insensibly toward that career of art which consists only in the tasting and recording of experience.

This, which is not so much a vocation for art as an impatience of all other honest trades, frequently exists alone; and so existing, it will pass gently away in the course of years. Emphatically, it is not to be regarded; it is not a vocation, but a temptation; and when your father the other day so fiercely and (in my view) so properly discouraged your ambition, he was recalling not improbably some similar passage in his own experience. For the temptation is perhaps nearly as common as the vocation is rare. But again we have vocations which are imperfect; we have men whose minds are bound up, not so much in any art, as in the general *ars artium* and common base of all creative work; who will now dip into painting, and now study counterpoint, and anon will be inditing a sonnet: all these with equal interest, all often with genuine knowledge. And of this temper, when it stands alone, I

find it difficult to speak; but I should counsel
such an one to take to letters, for in literature
(which drags with so wide a net) all his information may be found some day useful, and if
he should go on as he has begun, and turn at
last into the critic, he will have learned to use
the necessary tools. Lastly we come to those
vocations which are at once decisive and precise; to the men who are born with the love
of pigments, the passion of drawing, the gift of
music, or the impulse to create with words, just
as other and perhaps the same men are born
with the love of hunting, or the sea, or horses,
or the turning-lathe. These are predestined;
if a man love the labour of any trade, apart
from any question of success or fame, the gods
have called him. He may have the general
vocation too: he may have a taste for all the
arts, and I think he often has; but the mark
of his calling is this laborious partiality for
one, this inextinguishable zest in its technical
successes, and (perhaps above all) a certain
candour of mind, to take his very trifling
enterprise with a gravity that would befit the
cares of empire, and to think the smallest

improvement worth accomplishing at any expense of time and industry. The book, the statue, the sonata, must be gone upon with the unreasoning good faith and the un-flagging spirit of children at their play. *Is it worth doing?*—when it shall have occurred to any artist to ask himself that question, it is implicitly answered in the negative. It does not occur to the child as he plays at being a pirate on the dining-room sofa, nor to the hunter as he pursues his quarry; and the candour of the one and the ardour of the other should be united in the bosom of the artist.

If you recognise in yourself some such decisive taste, there is no room for hesitation: follow your bent. And observe (lest I should too much discourage you) that the disposition does not usually burn so brightly at the first, or rather not so constantly. Habit and prac-tice sharpen gifts; the necessity of toil grows less disgusting, grows even welcome, in the course of years; a small taste (if it be only genuine) waxes with indulgence into an ex-clusive passion. Enough, just now, if you can look back over a fair interval, and see that your chosen art has a little more than held its own among the thronging interests of youth. Time will do the rest, if devotion help it; and soon your every thought will be engrossed in that beloved occupation.

But even with devotion, you may remind me, even with unfaltering and delighted industry, many thousand artists spend their lives, if the result be regarded, utterly in vain: a thousand artists, and never one work of art. But the vast mass of mankind are incapable of doing anything reasonably well, art among the rest. The worthless artist would not improbably have been a quite incompetent baker. And the artist, even if he does not amuse the public, amuses himself; so that there will always be one man the happier for his vigils. This is the practical side of art: its inexpugnable fortress for the true practitioner. The direct returns—the wages of the trade—are small, but the indirect—the wages of the life—are incalculably great. No other business offers a man his daily bread upon such joyful terms. The soldier and the explorer have moments of a worthier excitement, but they are purchased by cruel hardships and periods of tedium that beggar language. In the life of the artist there need be no hour without its pleasure. I take the author, with whose career I am best acquainted; and it is true he works in a rebellious material, and that the act of writing is cramped and trying both to the eyes and the temper; but remark him in his study, when matter crowds upon him and words are not wanting—in what a continual series of small successes time flows by; with what a sense of power as of one moving mountains, he marshals his petty characters; with what pleasures, both of the ear and eye, he sees his airy structure growing on the page; and how he labours in a craft to which the whole material of his life is tributary, and which opens a door to all his tastes, his loves, his hatreds, and his convictions, so that what he writes is only what he longed to utter. He may have enjoyed many things in this big, tragic playground of the world; but what shall he have enjoyed more fully than a morning of successful work? Suppose it ill paid: the wonder is it should be paid at all. Other men pay, and pay dearly, for pleasures less desirable.

Nor will the practice of art afford you pleasure only; it affords besides an admirable training. For the artist works entirely upon honour. The public knows little or nothing of those merits in the quest of which you are condemned to spend the bulk of your endeavours. Merits of design, the merit of first-hand energy, the merit of a certain cheap accomplishment which a man of the artistic temper easily acquires—these they can recognise, and these they value. But to those more exquisite refinements of proficiency and finish, which the artist so ardently desires and so keenly feels, for which (in the vigorous words of Balzac) he must toil 'like a miner buried in a landslip,' for which, day after day, he recasts and revises and rejects—the gross mass of the public must be ever blind. To those lost pains, suppose you attain the highest pitch of merit, posterity may possibly do justice; suppose, as is so probable, you fail by even a hair's breadth of the highest, rest certain they shall never be observed.

Under the shadow of this cold thought, alone in his studio, the artist must preserve from day to day his constancy to the ideal. It is this which makes his life noble; it is by this that the practice of his craft strengthens and matures his character; it is for this that even the serious countenance of the great emperor was turned approvingly (if only for a moment) on the followers of Apollo, and that sternly gentle voice bade the artist cherish his art.

And here there fall two warnings to be made. First, if you are to continue to be a law to yourself, you must beware of the first signs of laziness. This idealism in honesty can only be supported by perpetual effort; the standard is easily lowered, the artist who says '*It will do,*' is on the down-ward path; three or four pot-boilers are enough at times (above all at wrong times) to falsify a talent, and by the practice of journalism a man runs the risk of becoming wedded to cheap finish. This is the danger on the one side; there is not less upon the other. The consciousness of how much the artist is (and must be) a law to himself, debauches the small heads. Perceiving recondite merits very hard to attain, making or swallowing artistic formulæ, or perhaps falling in love with some particular proficiency of his own, many artists forget the end of all art: to please. It is doubtless tempting to exclaim against the ignorant bourgeois; yet it should not be forgotten, it is he who is to pay us, and that (surely on the face of it) for services that he shall desire to have performed. Here also, if properly considered, there is a question of transcendental honesty. To give the public what they do not want, and yet expect to be supported: we have there a strange pretension, and yet not uncommon, above all with painters. The first duty in this world is for a man to pay his way; when that is quite accomplished, he may plunge into what eccentricity he likes; but emphatically not till then. Till then, he must pay assiduous court to the bourgeois who carries the purse. And if in the course of these capitulations he shall falsify his talent, it can never have been a strong one, and he will have preserved a better thing than talent—character. Or if he be of a mind so independent that he cannot stoop to this necessity, one course is yet open : he can desist from art, and follow some more manly way of life.

I speak of a more manly way of life, it is a point on which I must be frank. To live by a pleasure is not a high calling; it involves patronage, however veiled; it numbers the artist, however ambitious, along with dancing girls and billiard markers. The French have a romantic evasion for one employment, and call its practitioners the Daughters of Joy. The artist is of the same family, he is of the Sons of Joy, chose his trade to please himself, gains his livelihood by pleasing others, and has parted with something of the sterner dignity of man. Journals but a little while ago declaimed against the Tennyson peerage ; and this Son of Joy was blamed for condescension when he followed the example of Lord Lawrence and Lord Cairns and Lord Clyde. The poet was more happily inspired ; with a better modesty he accepted the honour ; and anonymous journalists have not yet (if I am to believe them) recovered the vicarious disgrace to their profession. When it comes to their turn, these gentlemen can do themselves more justice; and I shall be glad to think of it; for to my barbarian eyesight, even Lord Tennyson looks somewhat out of place in that assembly. There should be no honours for the artist; he has already, in the practice of his art, more than his share of the rewards of life; the honours are pre-empted for other trades, less agreeable and perhaps more useful.

But the devil in these trades of pleasing is to fail to please. In ordinary occupations, a man offers to do a certain thing or to produce a certain article with a merely conventional accomplishment, a design in which (we may almost say) it is difficult to fail. But the artist steps forth out of the crowd and proposes to delight: an impudent design, in which it is impossible to fail without odious circumstances. The poor Daughter of Joy, carrying her smiles and finery quite unregarded through the crowd, makes a figure which it is impossible to recall without a wounding pity. She is the type of the unsuccessful artist. The actor, the dancer, and the singer must appear like her in person, and drain publicly the cup of failure. But though the rest of us escape this crowning bitterness of the pillory, we all court in essence the same humiliation. We all profess to be able to delight. And how few of us are! We all pledge ourselves to be able to continue to delight. And the day will come to each, and even to the most admired, when the ardour shall have declined and the cunning shall be lost, and he shall sit by his deserted booth ashamed. Then shall he see himself condemned to do work for which he blushes to take payment. Then (as if his lot were not already cruel) he must lie exposed to the gibes of the wreckers of the press, who earn a little bitter bread by the condemnation of trash which they have not read, and the praise of excellence which they cannot understand.

And observe that this seems almost the necessary end at least of writers. *Les Blancs et les Bleus* (for instance) is of an order of merit very different from *Le Vicomte de Bragelonne ;* and if any gentleman can bear to spy upon the nakedness of *Castle Dangerous,* his name I think is Ham: let it be enough for the rest of us to read of it (not without tears) in the pages of Lockhart. Thus in old age, when occupation and comfort are most needful, the writer must lay aside at once his pastime and his breadwinner. The painter indeed, if he succeed at all in engaging the attention of the public, gains great sums and can stand to his easel until a great age without dishonourable failure. The writer has the double misfortune to be ill-paid while he can work, and to be incapable of working when he is old. It is thus a way of life which conducts directly to a false position.

For the writer (in spite of notorious examples to the contrary) must look to be ill-paid. Tennyson and Montépin make handsome livelihoods; but we cannot all hope to be Tennyson, and we do not all perhaps desire to be Montépin. If you adopt an art to be your trade, weed your mind at the outset of all desire of money. What you may decently expect, if you have some talent and much industry, is such an income as a clerk will earn with a tenth or perhaps a twentieth of your nervous output. Nor have you the right to look for more; in the wages of the life, not in the wages of the trade, lies your reward; the work is here the wages. It will be seen I have little sympathy with the common lamentations of the artist class. Perhaps they do not remember the hire of the field labourer; or do they think no parallel will lie? Perhaps they have never observed what is the retiring allowance of a field officer; or do they suppose their contributions to the arts of pleasing more important than the services of a colonel? Perhaps they forget on how little Millet was content to live; or do they think, because they have less genius, they stand excused from the display of equal virtues? But upon one point there should be no dubiety : if a man be not frugal, he has no business in the arts. If he be not frugal, he steers directly for that last tragic scene of *le vieux saltimbanque;* if he be not frugal, he will find it hard to continue to be honest. Some day, when the butcher is knocking at the door, he may be tempted, he may be obliged, to turn out and sell a slovenly piece of work. If the obligation shall have arisen through no wantonness of his own, he is even to be commended;

for words cannot describe how far more necessary it is that a man should support his family,
than that he should attain to—or preserve—
distinction in the arts. But if the pressure
comes through his own fault, he has stolen, and
stolen under trust, and stolen (which is the
worst of all) in such a way that no law can
reach him.

And now you may perhaps ask me, if the
debutant artist is to have no thought of money,
and if (as is implied) he is to expect no honours
from the State, he may not at least look forward
to the delights of popularity? Praise, you will
tell me, is a savoury dish. And in so far as you
may mean the countenance of other artists, you
would put your finger on one of the most
essential and enduring pleasures of the career
of art. But in so far as you should have an
eye to the commendations of the public or
the notice of the newspapers, be sure you would
but be cherishing a dream. It is true that in
certain esoteric journals the author (for instance)
is duly criticised, and that he is often praised a
great deal more than he deserves, sometimes for
qualities which he prided himself on eschewing,

and sometimes by ladies and gentlemen who
have denied themselves the privilege of reading
his work.   But if a man be sensitive to this
wild praise, we must suppose him equally alive
to that which often accompanies and always
follows it—wild ridicule.   A man may have
done well for years, and then he may fail; he
will hear of his failure.   Or he may have done
well for years, and still do well, but the critics
may have tired of praising him, or there may
have sprung up some new idol of the instant,
some 'dust a little gilt,' to whom they now prefer to offer sacrifice.   Here is the obverse and
the reverse of that empty and ugly thing called
popularity.   Will any man suppose it worth the
gaining?

XI

PULVIS ET UMBRA

WE look for some reward of our endeavours and are disappointed; not success, not happiness, not even peace of conscience, crowns our ineffectual efforts to do well. Our frailties are invincible, our virtues barren; the battle goes sore against us to the going down of the sun. The canting moralist tells us of right and wrong; and we look abroad, even on the face of our small earth, and find them change with every climate, and no country where some action is not honoured for a virtue and none where it is not branded for a vice; and we look in our experience, and find no vital congruity in the wisest rules, but at the best a municipal fitness. It is not strange if we are tempted to despair of good. We ask too much. Our religions and moralities have been trimmed to flatter us, till they are all emasculate and sentimentalised, and only please and weaken. Truth is of a rougher strain. In the harsh face of life, faith can read a bracing gospel. The human race is a thing more ancient than the ten commandments; and the bones and revolutions of the Kosmos, in whose joints we are but moss and fungus, more ancient still.

I

Of the Kosmos in the last resort, science reports many doubtful things and all of them appalling. There seems no substance to this solid globe on which we stamp: nothing but symbols and ratios. Symbols and ratios carry us and bring us forth and beat us down; gravity that swings the incommensurable suns and worlds through space, is but a figment varying inversely as the squares of distances; and the suns and worlds themselves, imponderable figures of abstraction, NH_3 and H_2O. Consideration dares not dwell upon this view; that way madness lies; 'science carries us into zones of speculation, where there is no habitable city for the mind of man.'

But take the Kosmos with a grosser faith, as our senses give it us. We behold space sown with rotatory islands, suns and worlds and the shards and wrecks of systems : some, like the sun, still blazing; some rotting, like the earth; others, like the moon, stable in desolation. All of these we take to be made of something we call matter : a thing which no analysis can help us to conceive; to whose incredible properties no familiarity can reconcile our minds. This stuff, when not purified by the lustration of fire, rots uncleanly into something we call life; seized through all its atoms with a pediculous malady; swelling in tumours that become independent, sometimes even (by an abhorrent prodigy) locomotory; one splitting into millions, millions cohering into one, as the malady proceeds through varying stages. This vital putrescence of the dust, used as we are to it, yet strikes us with occasional disgust, and the profusion of worms in a piece of ancient turf, or the air of a marsh darkened with insects, will sometimes check our breathing so that we aspire for cleaner places. But none is clean : the moving sand is infected with lice; the pure spring, where it bursts out of the mountain, is a mere issue of worms; even in the hard rock the crystal is forming.

In two main shapes this eruption covers the countenance of the earth: the animal and the vegetable: one in some degree the inversion of the other: the second rooted to the spot; the first coming detached out of its natal mud, and scurrying abroad with the myriad feet of insects or towering into the heavens on the wings of birds: a thing so inconceivable that, if it be well considered, the heart stops. To what passes with the anchored vermin, we have little clue: doubtless they have their joys and sorrows, their delights and killing agonies: it appears not how. But of the locomotory, to which we ourselves belong, we can tell more. These share with us a thousand miracles: the miracles of sight, of hearing, of the projection of sound, things that bridge space; the miracles of memory and reason, by which the present is conceived, and when it is gone, its image kept living in the brains of man and brute; the miracle of reproduction, with its imperious desires and staggering consequences. And to put the last touch upon this mountain mass of the revolting and the inconceivable, all these prey upon each other, lives tearing other lives in pieces, cramming them inside themselves, and by that summary process, growing fat : the vegetarian, the whale, perhaps the tree, not less than the lion of the desert; for the vegetarian is only the eater of the dumb.

Meanwhile our rotatory island loaded with predatory life, and more drenched with blood, both animal and vegetable, than ever mutinied ship, scuds through space with unimaginable speed, and turns alternate cheeks to the reverberation of a blazing world, ninety million miles away.

II

What a monstrous spectre is this man, the disease of the agglutinated dust, lifting alternate feet or lying drugged with slumber; killing, feeding, growing, bringing forth small copies of himself; grown upon with hair like grass, fitted with eyes that move and glitter in his face; a thing to set children screaming;—

and yet looked at nearlier, known as his fellows
know him, how surprising are his attributes!
Poor soul, here for so little, cast among so
many hardships, filled with desires so incom-
mensurate and so inconsistent, savagely surrounded, savagely descended, irremediably
condemned to prey upon his fellow lives:
who should have blamed him had he been of
a piece with his destiny and a being merely
barbarous? And we look and behold him
instead filled with imperfect virtues: infinitely
childish, often admirably valiant, often touch-
ingly kind; sitting down, amidst his momentary
life, to debate of right and wrong and the attributes of the deity; rising up to do battle for
an egg or die for an idea; singling out his
friends and his mate with cordial affection;
bringing forth in pain, rearing with long-
suffering solicitude, his young. To touch the
heart of his mystery, we find in him one
thought, strange to the point of lunacy: the
thought of duty; the thought of something
owing to himself, to his neighbour, to his
God: an ideal of decency, to which he would
rise if it were possible; a limit of shame, below

which, if it be possible, he will not stoop. The
design in most men is one of conformity; here
and there, in picked natures, it transcends itself
and soars on the other side, arming martyrs
with independence; but in all, in their degrees,
it is a bosom thought:—Not in man alone, for
we trace it in dogs and cats whom we know
fairly well, and doubtless some similar point of
honour sways the elephant, the oyster, and the
louse, of whom we know so little:—But in
man, at least, it sways with so complete an
empire that merely selfish things come second,
even with the selfish: that appetites are
starved, fears are conquered, pains supported;
that almost the dullest shrinks from the reproof
of a glance, although it were a child's; and all
but the most cowardly stand amid the risks
of war; and the more noble, having strongly
conceived an act as due to their ideal, affront
and embrace death. Strange enough if, with
their singular origin and perverted practice,
they think they are to be rewarded in some
future life: stranger still, if they are persuaded
of the contrary, and think this blow, which
they solicit, will strike them senseless for

eternity. I shall be reminded what a tragedy
of misconception and misconduct man at large
presents : of organised injustice, cowardly violence and treacherous crime; and of the damning imperfections of the best. They cannot
be too darkly drawn. /Man is indeed marked
for failure in his efforts to do right./ But
where the best consistently miscarry, how ten-
fold more remarkable that all should continue
to strive ; and surely we should find it both
touching and inspiriting, that in a field from
which success is banished, our race should not
cease to labour.

If the first view of this creature, stalking
in his rotatory isle, be a thing to shake the
courage of the stoutest, on this nearer sight,
he startles us with an admiring wonder. It
matters not where we look, under what climate
we observe him, in what stage of society, in
what depth of ignorance, burthened with what
erroneous morality ; by camp-fires in Assi-
niboia, the snow powdering his shoulders, the
wind plucking his blanket, as he sits, passing
the ceremonial calumet and uttering his grave
opinions like a Roman senator; in ships at sea,

a man inured to hardship and vile pleasures, his brightest hope a fiddle in a tavern and a bedizened trull who sells herself to rob him, and he for all that simple, innocent, cheerful, kindly like a child, constant to toil, brave to drown, for others; in the slums of cities, moving among indifferent millions to mechanical employments, without hope of change in the future, with scarce a pleasure in the present, and yet true to his virtues, honest up to his lights, kind to his neighbours, tempted perhaps in vain by the bright gin-palace, perhaps long-suffering with the drunken wife that ruins him; in India (a woman this time) kneeling with broken cries and streaming tears, as she drowns her child in the sacred river; in the brothel, the discard of society, living mainly on strong drink, fed with affronts, a fool, a thief, the comrade of thieves, and even here keeping the point of honour and the touch of pity, often repaying the world's scorn with service, often standing firm upon a scruple, and at a certain cost, rejecting riches :— everywhere some virtue cherished or affected, everywhere some decency of thought and

carriage, everywhere the ensign of man's ineffectual goodness :—ah! if I could show
you this! if I could show you these men
and women, all the world over, in every
stage of history, under every abuse of error,
under every circumstance of failure, without
hope, without help, without thanks, still ob-
scurely fighting the lost fight of virtue, still
clinging, in the brothel or on the scaffold, to
some rag of honour, the poor jewel of their
souls! They may seek to escape, and yet
they cannot; it is not alone their privilege
and glory, but their doom; they are condemned to some nobility; all their lives long,
the desire of good is at their heels, the im-
placable hunter.

Of all earth's meteors, here at least is the
most strange and consoling : that this ennobled
lemur, this hair-crowned bubble of the dust,
this inheritor of a few years and sorrows, should
yet deny himself his rare delights, and add to
his frequent pains, and live for an ideal, however
misconceived. Nor can we stop with man. A
new doctrine, received with screams a little
while ago by canting moralists, and still not

properly worked into the body of our thoughts, lights us a step farther into the heart of this rough but noble universe. For nowadays the pride of man denies in vain his kinship with the original dust. He stands no longer like a thing apart. Close at his heels we see the dog, prince of another genus: and in him too, we see dumbly testified the same cultus of an unattainable ideal, the same constancy in failure. Does it stop with the dog? We look at our feet where the ground is blackened with the swarming ant: a creature so small, so far from us in the hierarchy of brutes, that we can scarce trace and scarce comprehend his doings; and here also, in his ordered polities and rigorous justice, we see confessed the law of duty and the fact of individual sin. Does it stop, then, with the ant? Rather this desire of well-doing and this doom of frailty run through all the grades of life: rather is this earth, from the frosty top of Everest to the next margin of the internal fire, one stage of ineffectual virtues and one temple of pious tears and perseverance. The whole creation groaneth and travaileth together. It is the common and the god-like

law of life. The browsers, the biters, the
barkers, the hairy coats of field and forest, the
squirrel in the oak, the thousand-footed creeper
in the dust, as they share with us the gift of
life, share with us the love of an ideal: strive
like us—like us are tempted to grow weary of
the struggle—to do well; like us receive at
times unmerited refreshment, visitings of support, returns of courage; and are condemned
like us to be crucified between that double law
of the members and the will. Are they like us,
I wonder, in the timid hope of some reward,
some sugar with the drug? do they, too, stand
aghast at unrewarded virtues, at the sufferings
of those whom, in our partiality, we take to be
just, and the prosperity of such as, in our blindness, we call wicked? It may be, and yet God
knows what they should look for. Even while
they look, even while they repent, the foot of
man treads them by thousands in the dust, the
yelping hounds burst upon their trail, the bullet
speeds, the knives are heating in the den of the
vivisectionist; or the dew falls, and the generation of a day is blotted out. For these are
creatures, compared with whom our weakness is

strength, our ignorance wisdom, our brief span eternity.

And as we dwell, we living things, in our isle of terror and under the imminent hand of death, God forbid it should be man the erected, the reasoner, the wise in his own eyes—God forbid it should be man that wearies in well-doing, that despairs of unrewarded effort, or utters the language of complaint. Let it be enough for faith, that the whole creation groans in mortal frailty, strives with unconquerable constancy: Surely not all in vain.

XII

A CHRISTMAS SERMON

By the time this paper appears, I shall have been talking for twelve months;[1] and it is thought I should take my leave in a formal and seasonable manner.   Valedictory eloquence is rare, and death-bed sayings have not often hit the mark of the occasion.   Charles Second, wit and sceptic, a man whose life had been one long lesson in human incredulity, an easy-going comrade, a manœuvring king—remembered and embodied all his wit and scepticism along with more than his usual good humour in the famous 'I am afraid, gentlemen, I am an unconscionable time a-dying.'

I

An unconscionable time a-dying—there is the picture ('I am afraid, gentlemen,') of your

---

[1] *i.e.* in the pages of *Scribner's Magazine* (1888).

life and of mine. The sands run out, and the
hours are 'numbered and imputed,' and the
days go by; and when the last of these finds
us, we have been a long time dying, and what
else? The very length is something, if we reach
that hour of separation undishonoured; and to
have lived at all is doubtless (in the soldierly
expression) to have served. There is a tale in
Tacitus of how the veterans mutinied in the
German wilderness; of how they mobbed Ger-
manicus, clamouring to go home; and of how,
seizing their general's hand, these old, war-worn
exiles passed his finger along their toothless
gums. *Sunt lacrymæ rerum:* this was the most
eloquent of the songs of Simeon. And when a
man has lived to a fair age, he bears his marks
of service. He may have never been remarked
upon the breach at the head of the army; at
least he shall have lost his teeth on the camp
bread.

The idealism of serious people in this age
of ours is of a noble character. It never
seems to them that they have served enough;
they have a fine impatience of their virtues.
It were perhaps more modest to be singly

thankful that we are no worse. It is not only our enemies, those desperate characters—it is we ourselves who know not what we do;— thence springs the glimmering hope that perhaps we do better than we think: that to scramble through this random business with hands reasonably clean, to have played the part of a man or woman with some reasonable fulness, to have often resisted the diabolic, and at the end to be still resisting it, is for the poor human soldier to have done right well. To ask to see some fruit of our endeavour is but a transcendental way of serving for reward; and what we take to be contempt of self is only greed of hire.

And again if we require so much of ourselves, shall we not require much of others? If we do not genially judge our own deficiencies, is it not to be feared we shall be even stern to the trespasses of others? And he who (looking back upon his own life) can see no more than that he has been unconscionably long a-dying, will he not be tempted to think his neighbour unconscionably long of getting hanged? It is probable that nearly all who

think of conduct at all, think of it too much;
it is certain we all think too much of sin.　We
are not damned for doing wrong, but for not
doing right;　Christ would never hear of
negative morality;　*thou shalt* was ever his
word, with which he superseded *thou shalt not.*
To make our idea of morality centre on forbidden acts is to defile the imagination and to
introduce into our judgments of our fellow-men
a secret element of gusto.　If a thing is wrong
for us, we should not dwell upon the thought
of it;　or we shall soon dwell upon it with
inverted pleasure.　If we cannot drive it from
our minds—one thing of two:　either our
creed is in the wrong and we must more in-
dulgently remodel it;　or else, if our morality
be in the right, we are criminal lunatics and
should place our persons in restraint.　A mark
of such unwholesomely divided minds is the
passion for interference with others:　the Fox
without the Tail was of this breed, but had
(if his biographer is to be trusted) a certain
antique civility now out of date.　A man may
have a flaw, a weakness, that unfits him for
the duties of life, that spoils his temper, that

threatens his integrity, or that betrays him into cruelty. It has to be conquered; but it must never be suffered to engross his thoughts. The true duties lie all upon the farther side, and must be attended to with a whole mind so soon as this preliminary clearing of the decks has been effected. In order that he may be kind and honest, it may be needful he should become a total abstainer; let him become so then, and the next day let him forget the circumstance. Trying to be kind and honest will require all his thoughts; a mortified appetite is never a wise companion; in so far as he has had to mortify an appetite, he will still be the worse man; and of such an one a great deal of cheerfulness will be required in judging life, and a great deal of humility in judging others.

It may be argued again that dissatisfaction with our life's endeavour springs in some degree from dulness. We require higher tasks, because we do not recognise the height of those we have. Trying to be kind and honest seems an affair too simple and too inconsequential for gentlemen of our heroic mould;

we had rather set ourselves to something bold, arduous, and conclusive; we had rather found a schism or suppress a heresy, cut off a hand or mortify an appetite. But the task before us, which is to co-endure with our existence, is rather one of microscopic fineness, and the heroism required is that of patience. There is no cutting of the Gordian knots of life; each must be smilingly unravelled.

To be honest, to be kind—to earn a little and to spend a little less, to make upon the whole a family happier for his presence, to renounce when that shall be necessary and not be embittered, to keep a few friends but these without capitulation—above all, on the same grim condition, to keep friends with himself—here is a task for all that a man has of fortitude and delicacy. He has an ambitious soul who would ask more; he has a hopeful spirit who should look in such an enterprise to be successful. There is indeed one element in human destiny that not blindness itself can controvert: whatever else we are intended to do, we are not intended to succeed; failure is the fate allotted. It is so in every art and

study; it is so above all in the continent art
of living well. Here is a pleasant thought for
the year's end or for the end of life: Only self-
deception will be satisfied, and there need be
no despair for the despairer.

II

But Christmas is not only the mile-mark of
another year, moving us to thoughts of self-
examination: it is a season, from all its associations, whether domestic or religious, suggesting
thoughts of joy. A man dissatisfied with his
endeavours is a man tempted to sadness. And
in the midst of the winter, when his life runs
lowest and he is reminded of the empty chairs
of his beloved, it is well he should be condemned
to this fashion of the smiling face. Noble disappointment, noble self-denial are not to be
admired, not even to be pardoned, if they bring
bitterness. It is one thing to enter the kingdom
of heaven maim; another to maim yourself and
stay without. And the kingdom of heaven is
of the childlike, of those who are easy to please,

who love and who give pleasure. Mighty men of their hands, the smiters and the builders and the judges, have lived long and done sternly and yet preserved this lovely character; and among our carpet interests and twopenny concerns, the shame were indelible if *we* should lose it. Gentleness and cheerfulness, these come before all morality; they are the perfect duties. And it is the trouble with moral men that they have neither one nor other. It was the moral man, the Pharisee, whom Christ could not away with. If your morals make you dreary, depend upon it they are wrong. I do not say 'give them up,' for they may be all you have; but conceal them like a vice, lest they should spoil the lives of better and simpler people.

A strange temptation attends upon man: to keep his eye on pleasures, even when he will not share in them; to aim all his morals against them. This very year a lady (singular icono-clast!) proclaimed a crusade against dolls; and the racy sermon against lust is a feature of the age. I venture to call such moralists insincere. At any excess or perversion of a natural appetite, their lyre sounds of itself with relish-

ing denunciations; but for all displays of the
truly diabolic—envy, malice, the mean lie, the
mean silence, the calumnious truth, the back-
biter, the petty tyrant, the peevish poisoner of
family life—their standard is quite different.
These are wrong, they will admit, yet somehow
not so wrong; there is no zeal in their assault
on them, no secret element of gusto warms up
the sermon; it is for things not wrong in themselves that they reserve the choicest of their
indignation.   A man may naturally disclaim
all moral kinship with the Reverend Mr. Zola
or the hobgoblin old lady of the dolls; for
these are gross and naked instances. And yet
in each of us some similar element resides. The
sight of a pleasure in which we cannot or else
will not share moves us to a particular impatience.   It may be because we are envious, or
because we are sad, or because we dislike noise
and romping—being so refined, or because—
being so philosophic—we have an overweighing
sense of life's gravity: at least, as we go on in
years, we are all tempted to frown upon our
neighbour's pleasures.   People are nowadays
so fond of resisting temptations; here is one to

be resisted. They are fond of self-denial; here is a propensity that cannot be too peremptorily denied. There is an idea abroad among moral people that they should make their neighbours good. One person I have to make good: myself. But my duty to my neighbour is much more nearly expressed by saying that I have to make him happy—if I may.

III

Happiness and goodness, according to canting moralists, stand in the relation of effect and cause. There was never anything less proved or less probable: our happiness is never in our own hands; we inherit our constitution; we stand buffet among friends and enemies; we may be so built as to feel a sneer or an aspersion with unusual keenness, and so circumstanced as to be unusually exposed to them; we may have nerves very sensitive to pain, and be afflicted with a disease very painful. Virtue will not help us, and it is not meant to help us. It is not even its own reward, except for the self-

centred and—I had almost said—the unam-
iable. No man can pacify his conscience; if
quiet be what he want, he shall do better to let
that organ perish from disuse. And to avoid the
penalties of the law, and the minor *capitis dimi-
nutio* of social ostracism, is an affair of wisdom
—of cunning, if you will—and not of virtue.

In his own life, then, a man is not to expect
happiness, only to profit by it gladly when it
shall arise; he is on duty here; he knows not
how or why, and does not need to know; he
knows not for what hire, and must not ask.
Somehow or other, though he does not know
what goodness is, he must try to be good;
somehow or other, though he cannot tell what
will do it, he must try to give happiness to
others. And no doubt there comes in here a
frequent clash of duties. How far is he to
make his neighbour happy? How far must he
respect that smiling face, so easy to cloud, so
hard to brighten again? And how far, on the
other side, is he bound to be his brother's
keeper and the prophet of his own morality?
How far must he resent evil?

The difficulty is that we have little guidance ; Christ's sayings on the point being hard to reconcile with each other, and (the most of them) hard to accept. But the truth of his teaching would seem to be this : in our own person and fortune, we should be ready to accept and to pardon all ; it is *our* cheek we are to turn, *our* coat that we are to give away to the man who has taken *our* cloak. But when another's face is buffeted, perhaps a little of the lion will become us best. That we are to suffer others to be injured, and stand by, is not conceivable and surely not desirable. Revenge, says Bacon, is a kind of wild justice ; its judgments at least are delivered by an insane judge ; and in our own quarrel we can see nothing truly and do nothing wisely. But in the quarrel of our neighbour, let us be more bold. One person's happiness is as sacred as another's ; when we cannot defend both, let us defend one with a stout heart. It is only in so far as we are doing this, that we have any right to interfere : the defence of B is our only ground of action against A. A has as good a right to go to the devil, as we to go to glory ; and neither knows what he does

The truth is that all these interventions and denunciations and militant mongerings of moral half-truths, though they be sometimes needful, though they are often enjoyable, do yet belong to an inferior grade of duties. Ill-temper and envy and revenge find here an arsenal of pious disguises; this is the playground of inverted lusts. With a little more patience and a little less temper, a gentler and wiser method might be found in almost every case; and the knot that we cut by some fine heady quarrel-scene in private life, or, in public affairs, by some de-nunciatory act against what we are pleased to call our neighbour's vices, might yet have been unwoven by the hand of sympathy.

IV

To look back upon the past year, and see how little we have striven and to what small purpose; and how often we have been cowardly and hung back, or temerarious and rushed un-wisely in; and how every day and all day long we have transgressed the law of kindness;—it may seem a paradox, but in the bitterness of these discoveries, a certain consolation resides. Life is not designed to minister to a man's vanity. He goes upon his long business most of the time with a hanging head, and all the time like a blind child. Full of rewards and pleasures as it is—so that to see the day break or the moon rise, or to meet a friend, or to hear the dinner-call when he is hungry, fills him with surprising joys—this world is yet for him no abiding city. Friendships fall through, health fails, weariness assails him; year after year, he must thumb the hardly varying record of his own weakness and folly. It is a friendly process of detachment. When the time comes that he should go, there need be few illusions left about himself. *Here lies one who meant well, tried a little, failed much:*—surely that may be his epitaph, of which he need not be ashamed. Nor will he complain at the summons which calls a defeated soldier from the field: defeated, ay, if he were Paul or Marcus Aurelius! —but if there is still one inch of fight in his old spirit, undishonoured. The faith which sustained him in his life-long blindness and life-long disappointment will scarce even be required in this last formality of laying down his arms. Give him a march with his old bones; there, out of the glorious sun-coloured earth, out of the day and the dust and the ecstasy—there goes another Faithful Failure!

From a recent book of verse, where there is more than one such beautiful and manly poem, I take this memorial piece: it says better than I can, what I love to think; let it be our parting word.

'A late lark twitters from the quiet skies;
  And from the west,
  Where the sun, his day's work ended,
  Lingers as in content,
  There falls on the old, gray city
  An influence luminous and serene,
  A shining peace.

'The smoke ascends
  In a rosy-and-golden haze.   The spires
  Shine, and are changed.   In the valley
  Shadows rise.   The lark sings on.   The sun,
  Closing his benediction,
  Sinks, and the darkening air
  Thrills with a sense of the triumphing night—
  Night, with her train of stars
  And her great gift of sleep.

'So be my passing !
My task accomplished and the long day done,
My wages taken, and in my heart
Some late lark singing,
Let me be gathered to the quiet west,
The sundown splendid and serene,
Death.'[1]

---

[1] From *A Book of Verses* by William Ernest Henley.
D. Nutt, 1888.

[1888.]

THE WORKS OF
ROBERT LOUIS STEVENSON

The Letters of Robert Louis Stevenson.

Edited by SIDNEY COLVIN.   With drawings by PEIXOTTO and GUÉRIN.   2 vols., 8vo, $5.00 *net*.

The following volumes, 12mo, red cloth, 25 volumes,
in a box, $32.00.

St. Ives.

The Adventures of a French Prisoner in England.   12mo, $1.50.

"St. Ives" is a story of action and adventure in the author's most buoyant and stirring manner.   One does not expect to find commonplaces in Stevenson, but even his most ardent admirers may well be surprised at the grim tragedy in the opening chapters of "St. Ives."

In the South Seas.

With Map.   12mo, $1.50.

This volume is made up of selections from the interesting sketches contributed to periodicals by Mr. Stevenson, narrating his experiences and observations in the Marquesas (the scene of Melville's "Typee"), Paumotus, and the Gilbert Islands, gathered in the course of two cruises on the yacht "Casco" (1888) and the schooner "Equator" (1889).

Weir of Hermiston.

12mo, $1.50.

"Surely no son of Scotland has died, leaving with his last breath a worthier tribute to the land he loved."—SIDNEY COLVIN.

Poems and Ballads.

12mo, $1.50.

Comprising all the poems contained in "A Child's Garden of Verses," "Ballads," "Underwoods," and, in addition, over forty pieces of verse written since the publication of these volumes.

Kidnapped.

Being Memoirs of the Adventures of David Balfour in the year 1751. With 16 full-page illustrations by William Hole.   12mo, $1.50.

"Mr. Stevenson has never appeared to greater advantage than in 'Kidnapped.' No better book of its kind has ever been written."—*The Nation.*

David Balfour.

Being Memoirs of his Adventures at Home and Abroad.   12mo, $1.50.

"Surely the rarest and noblest work of fiction in the English language produced in the year."—*New York Times.*

Treasure Island.

A Story of the Spanish Main.   Illustrated.   12mo, $1.00.

"Primarily it is a book for boys, but it is a book which will be delightful to all grown men who have the sentiment of treasure hunting. . . Like all Mr. Stevenson's good work, it is touched with genius. . . . A masterpiece of narrative."
—*The Saturday Review.*

Virginibus Puerisque,

And Other Papers. 12mo, $1.25.

" Avowedly the book of a young man taking account of life from the starting point. There is a great deal in it which is individual, suggestive, and direct from life. There are sayings about Truth of Intercourse which penetrate a long way. There are passages concerning youth which probe to the quick some of its ailments and errors."—*Atlantic Monthly.*

Memories and Portraits.

12mo, $1.25.

" The grace and delicacy, the just artistic instinct, the curious aptness of phrase which distinguish these essays, can be fully appreciated only by a reader who loves to go back to them again and again after a first perusal."—*Lippincott's Magazine.*

Memoir of Fleeming Jenkin.

12mo, $1.25.

" The glimpses that we get of Mr. Stevenson himself in this book are charming and add greatly to its edifying and entertaining character. The style of the narrative is original, lucid, and spirited."—*Boston Saturday Evening Gazette.*

Familiar Studies of Men and Books.

12mo, $1.25.

CONTENTS: Victor Hugo's Romances, Some Aspects of Robert Burns, Walt Whitman, Henry David Thoreau, Yoshida Torajiro, Francois Villon, Charles of Orleans, Samuel Pepys, John Knox, and Women.

An Inland Voyage.

12mo, $1.00.

" Mr. Stevenson does not make canoeing itself his main theme, but delights in charming bits of description that, in their close attention to picturesque detail, remind one of the work of a skilled 'genre' painter. Nor does he hesitate . . . . to indulge in a strain of gently humorous reflection that furnishes some of the pleasantest passages of the book."—*Good Literature.*

Travels with a Donkey

In the Cévennes. 12mo, $1.00.

" The author sees everything with the eye of a philosopher. He has a steady flow of humor that is as apparently spontaneous as a mountain brook, and he views a landscape or a human figure, not only as a tourist seeking subjects for a book, but as an artist to whom the slightest line or tint carries a definite impression."—*Boston Courier.*

The Silverado Squatters.

With a frontispiece by Walter Crane. 12mo, $1.00.

" The interest of the book centres in graphic style and keen observation of the author. He has the power of describing places and characters with such vividness that you seem to have made personal acquaintance with both."—*N. Y. World.*

Across the Plains.

With Other Memories and Essays. 12mo, $1.25.

" The book sets us again to wondering at the facility with which Mr. Stevenson makes phrases and builds paragraphs ; moreover, we renew our admiration for a style as subtle as ether and as brilliant as fire opal."—*The Independent.*

A Foot-Note to History.

Eight Years of Trouble in Samoa. 12mo, $1.50.

"A story well worth reading. We have first a description of the curious and complex elements of discord, both native and foreign, in Samoa, and then a marvelous story of how these discordant elements have been at work during eight years."—*Public Opinion.*